Just Nuts

Allen Gilbert

HYLAND HOUSE

First published in Australia in 2005 by
Hyland House Publishing Pty Ltd
PO Box 122
Flemington
Victoria 3031

National Library of Australia
Cataloguing-in-publication data:

Gilbert, Allen.
    Just nuts.

    Bibliography.
    Includes index.
    ISBN 1 86447 091 7.

    1. Nuts – Australia. I. Title.

634.50994

Edited by Betty Moore
Layout and Design by Rob Cowpe Design
Printed by Everbest, China

Contents

Acknowledgments

First and foremost I wish to thank my partner, Laurie Cosgrove, for her input without which this book would never have been written.

Thanks, too, to the Victorian Department of Agriculture for the employment opportunity lasting over twenty-two years which helped gather much of this information.

The IPPS (International Plant Propagators Society) is an organisation that gets little press, but the conferences, contacts made and particularly field trips in different States that I have attended have added much to the information gathered in this book.

Mr Ting, formerly manager of Friendly Travel Service, deserves special mention as it was through him that I had the opportunity to travel many times to China and gather invaluable horticultural information.

I wish to thank Michael Schoo of Hyland House for suggesting this book; and the Hyland House editor, Bet Moore, for her work.

Some people contributed photographs and I acknowledge their help, in particular Cynthia Carson, Senior Extension Horticulturist, Manager Grow Help Australia, DPI&F, Queensland; Lindy Lahn, Lahnlea Quondongs, Moulamein, NSW; Ian Crosthwaite, Senior Agronomist, BGA Agriservices, Queensland; and Dr Roger Spencer, Horticultural Botanist, National Herbarium of Victoria, Royal Botanic Gardens, Melbourne, Victoria.

The drawings of the Brazil nut are based on photographs by H.F. Macmillan on page 445 of *A Gardener's Chronicle*, 1908.

The following organisations and individuals also made valuable contributions: Raoul & Suzie Copalov, Caufield, Victoria; CSR, Queensland; Geoffrey Dodd, Trawella Pecan Plantations, NSW; John and Sue Elliot, Narre Warren North, Victoria; Keith Harris, Clayton, Victoria; Bruce Hedge, Newham, Victoria; John Hunt, Seville, Victoria; Brian and Julie Hurse, Carisbrook, Victoria; Essie Huxley, Longley, Tasmania; Philomena Kenny, Parkdale, Victoria; Jim and Marina Martin, 'Ye Medieval Herb Garden', Mildura, Victoria; Reg and Lucy Packer, Swan Hill Chemicals, Swan Hill, Victoria; Gerry Reid, Bruny Island Tasmania; Rippon Lea National Trust Gardens, Elsternwick, Victoria; Margaret Vane, Elsternwick, Victoria; Alexandria Volkov, Brighton East, Victoria; Craig West, West Footscray, Victoria; and Peter Young, Birdwood Nursery, Nambour, Queensland.

I apologise, should anyone have been forgotten in these acknowledgments. Many, many home gardeners and professional people have helped me with ideas, information, and photographs; others allowed grafting and pruning experiments to be done on their nut trees and let me take photographs, some of which are used in this book.

Introduction

The word 'nut' comes from the Latin 'nutriens', to nourish, and nuts truly do this. Most are high in calories, rich in fats and proteins and contain varying amounts of carbohydrate, minerals and vitamins. Some nuts have important traces of essential elements such as selenium, vital to human nutrition and health. Nuts are an important, and in some cases an essential, part of the diet of most people of the world. Edible tree nuts directly provide many food items, including oils, spices, condiments and drinks, and are an important ingredient in many others.

Edible tree nuts and their by-products contribute in many ways to our daily lives. Nut oils have a number of industrial uses, such as in paints, varnishes, soaps and perfumes, and may also be used for culinary purposes. Nut trees provide beautiful woods often prized for their grain and durability. By-products, the shells and husks, are used as fuel in some parts of the world but some have industrial uses as well. Pecan and walnut shells, for example, are ground extremely finely to degrease aircraft engines, while finely ground pecan shells provide ingredients for carpet cleaners. Ground husks and shells are also used in poultry and animal litter, in stock feed, in garden and farm fertilisers, as mulches and growing media for plants, and for fine abrasives in soaps and metal polishes. Fillers for plastic wood, adhesives and non-slip surface paints can also contain dried and ground nut shells and husks. Bark and wood extracts from some nuts are used in leather tanning processes and parts of some nut flowers contribute to dying silks and are used as mordants.

Like berries, nuts are one of the oldest forage foods. They were relatively easy for early hunter gatherers to collect, store and carry and have remained an important food source and basis for recipes of many cultures. Evidence of very early human use of nuts has been found at archeological sites in many parts of the world. Their spread around the world was facilitated by early human movement, such that the exact origins of some species such as the walnut have been lost in time.

While nuts are such a common part of daily life that they are often taken for granted, it is sometimes difficult to say just which plants should be included in the category 'nuts'. There are two classic definitions, but many other attempts are made at categorising. Nut have been defined as single-seeded, hard-shelled, dry fruit. Macadamias, pistachios, sweet chestnuts, almonds and hazelnuts fit this definition. Nuts are also, however, sometimes defined very broadly as any seed or fruit that contains an edible kernel within a hard shell. Walnuts, pecans, cashews, coconuts and brazil nuts can be included under this definition, as can peanuts. (While the peanut is a legume it is usually considered a nut.) There are a number of other food items that might be regarded as 'seeds' rather than nuts, but which might also be included in this second very broad definition. Sunflowers, for example, might be defined as nuts rather than seeds and are sometimes included in the category, as are poppy seeds.

Defining and categorising nuts, therefore, is not as simple a matter as it might seem. As this is a book for the home gardener I have organised it to include macadamias, pistachios, sweet chestnuts, almonds and hazelnuts as well as walnuts, pecans, cashews, coconuts and brazil nuts in a section on tree nuts. Peanuts I have included in the section on other edible nuts. Not all of the nuts in this latter section are a part of our regular diet, nor are they generally regarded as true nuts, but they are interesting plants with some claim to be included in a book dealing with nuts. They include ginkgo, quandongs and water chestnuts, and the Bunya Bunya pine which has been used by Australian indigenous people as a food source. Other nuts such as Indian almond are also included in this section. Many of them have potential for use in the home garden and most are not well covered in other horticultural works.

Edible tree nuts are amongst the oldest flora of the world and are found on most continents of the Earth. In fact there is probably a nut-producing plant suitable for almost every major climatic region except the north and south poles. Nut-producing plants have, in times of famine, kept some populations alive and the products of various nut trees enhanced early human quality of life. Interest has increased in producing nuts for food, as well as their nutritional value in modern day diets. Most of the major nut tree species are now being grown in Australia and research is being undertaken to upgrade those existing as well as to find new cultivars and new ways of growing and producing nuts more economically.

Australia has its own edible tree nut, the macadamia, which is fast becoming an important commercial species around the world. Most of the other tree nuts grow well in one part or another of the Australian

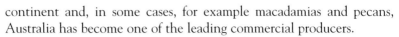

continent and, in some cases, for example macadamias and pecans, Australia has become one of the leading commercial producers.

Many tree nuts depend on grafting cultivars so a comprehensive section on budding and grafting is included as well as another on other means of propagation. Pruning, including my own minimal pruning approach, is also dealt with separately.

Each of the sections discussing specific nuts covers the pests and diseases that may affect that nut. These mostly entered Australia accidentally in the past by means of infected material, and this shows how easy it was to introduce troublesome pests and diseases. Had more awareness existed then of their potential impact, Australia today could have been relatively free of those that elsewhere affect plant species, especially fruit crops. Unfortunately, as this is not so, pest and disease control remains an essential part of growing crops such as nuts. Thankfully, quarantine inspections and import restrictions now prevent the entry of many further devastating pests and diseases affecting nut species.

I advocate organic farming and gardening so I have emphasised organic control methods. Organics is generally defined as gardening and farming by using recyclable and natural resouces which do the least harm to the environment, caring for the soil by increasing biological activity within it, and improving soil structure and soil health. Growing tree nuts as well as other nuts is relatively easy using organic, chemical-free approaches.

Of the many pests and diseases affecting nut producing trees, most can be controlled with good management and the use of organically recommended materials. Chemical methods of control are also available.

Nuts of all kinds lend themselves to permaculture enterprises; not only do they provide foods of many kinds but they also contribute in a number of other ways: they can be grown as part of a self-sufficiency oriented food farming or gardening enterprise for shade, foliage, husks for mulch and poultry litter, and for diet, including high protein diet for vegetarians and vegans.

Storage of nuts is very important and each section deals with particular storing issues. Nuts generally contain high levels of oil so they can easily beome rancid. How long they stay fresh depends on how much oil they contain. Generally they should be stored in cool, dark places or in the refrigerator. They can be kept for longer periods (up to one year) in the freezer. Because of their high moisture content some nuts are also particularly susceptible to moulds so it is important that they be stored in dry, airtight containers in cool, dark places.

A comprehensive glossary is followed by a section providing suggestions for further reading, as well as lists of additional resources for the home gardener.

TREE NUTS

their cultivation and uses

Almonds

P r u n u s   d u l c i s

Almonds (family *Rosaceae*) were first brought to Australia during the early settlement years, and used mainly as windbreaks. In *The Fruitgrower's Handbook* in 1913 McEwin writes: 'The almond, like the fig, is principally planted in fence lines and waste corners, as windbreaks and orchard shelter, and does not receive an overplus of attention in the manner of pruning or cultivation.' In the courtyard of the old Richmond gaol in Richmond, Tasmania, there is still standing one giant tree that could be over 100 years old.

The first commercial plantings of almonds in orchards were recorded in South Australia and Western Australia during the early 1900s. Emphasis was placed on planting different cultivars for effective pollination, as it was thought at the time that the almond was self-infertile (that is, one tree cannot pollinate itself), and had separate male and female flowers that opened at slightly different times. The 1921 (third) edition of the WA Department of Agriculture's *Handbook of Horticulture and Viticulture of Western Australia* points out that 'the majority of almonds bear two classes of flowers: the female and the male. These issue at some days' interval, and at times so early in the spring, as to fail to set on account of light frost or of defective pollination.' It is now known that the almond does not have separate male and female flowers but the flowers are self-infertile and need cross pollination (pollen from another tree) to produce fruit successfully.

Commercial almond plantings eventually spread to north-western Victoria and New South Wales, particularly in areas with long, hot, dry, summers, cool but mild winters and where frost-free spring conditions prevailed and where irrigation water was available. Large plantations now exist in several areas including the Sunraysia region of Victoria. South Australian almond production areas have increased and are now spreading to the Barossa Valley, Adelaide Plains, Willunga and Riverland regions.

Care and maintenance

Almonds grow into largish trees of about 9 m. Some cultivars such as 'Brand's Jordan' seem to have very upright growth and the wood of all almonds is very strong, solid, hard and stringy. In fact, since almond wood is probably the toughest of all stone fruits to cut, any pruning system that reduces the amount of required pruning is a blessing in disguise. An alternative is to do any necessary pruning during the soft growth period in summer, an option many gardeners adhere to with all types of stone fruits, including almonds.

Because most almonds are self-infertile, it is necessary to plant two trees of different cultivars for pollination purposes. The usual spacing of pollinator trees is about one in ten. The problem of finding space for two trees can be overcome by planting two in the one hole or by grafting or budding a pollinator onto one branch of a single tree. It is possible sometimes to buy multi-grafted trees which will also solve the pollination problem.

There is one cultivar on the market that is self-fertile; it is called 'All-in-One'. I have a tree of this cultivar that I have trained as a fan-shaped espalier against a fence to save space. It is now beginning to fruit in its third season, but with only a handful of nuts. New plant breeding programs are active and are aimed at breeding self-pollinating, soft-shelled almond cultivars.

It is essential that almond trees are planted into soil that is well drained. A handful of organic fertiliser such as fowl manure can be placed in the base of the hole, then covered with about 100 mm of soil. The tree can then be planted into the hole making sure that the roots do not come into contact with the fertiliser. Once the hole is filled and the tree planted the soil should be only lightly tamped and then the whole area watered to make sure all air has been expelled from air pockets in the planting hole. After a few hours, water again with a liquid seaweed product such as Maxicrop™: this will encourage fibrous roots to develop quickly. To overcome problems with heavy soils that are prone to water logging, plant the trees into large above-ground mounds.

Young nursery bought trees are usually single-branched or of a vase shape featuring 4-5 branches, these usually having been pruned so that they remain about 300 mm long. To obtain a well-shaped tree that grows into a low profile shape rather than a tall, upright tree it is very important to develop many branches on the tree as soon as possible. Ideally, the branches of the young tree should be winter pruned to about

Almond seedling
(bitter almond)
(*Prunus dulcis*)
with pink blossom

100 mm with two sideways-facing buds at the top of the cut branch. Any strong buds inside the vase shape that would grow into the centre of the tree can be removed with a knife or secateur blade as these buds would grow too strongly and create 'water shoots' that would have to be removed at a later date. If the young tree has four branches, then pruning back to two buds on each should allow two more new branches to grow from the end of each original branch, so that if left to grow until the autumn–winter period the plant should have developed eight branches. This is the stage that traditional pruning aims for — to have about eight main limbs in a vase shape to develop strong branches that will carry heavy crops of fruit/nuts. Trees left virtually unpruned from this stage forward develop into well-branched open trees that need little pruning; they do, however, eventually grow fairly tall.

The single-branched nursery tree can be pruned hard to begin the pruning system described above, or left unpruned. A single-branched tree left unpruned will develop a central leader pyramid shape; this is an option for gardeners. Trees left to develop the central leader system often become rather crowded with limbs after about 8–9 years and at this stage they can have the centre removed to near the base, which will leave a tree of perfect vase shape that is more open and easier to manage.

I have developed my own pruning system, whereby it is necessary to prune each of the eight limbs (see above) created from the first pruning back to 100-200 mm instead of leaving them unpruned, thus causing a doubling up of limbs, again giving 16 or more limbs by the next winter. In fact, I recommend that summer pruning be carried out when developing the young tree so that during one year the branch number is doubled twice. Summer pruning can be done in the November–December period when each growing branch shoot is cut back to about 100 mm. At each site two more branches will start to grow which will give another doubling of branch numbers by the end of the growth season.

The main aim of my own pruning system is to develop about 20–30 limbs on the young trees. If summer pruning is used, this can be achieved in two years from planting. Once the desired number of limbs has been created then no more pruning is necessary for several years, except to prune out dead or diseased limbs, and any water shoots (see Glossary) growing into the centre of the tree. By using this pruning system trees will remain small and low growing which is ideal for home gardens, easier for picking, pruning and spraying operations; low growing trees are easier to net to stop birds eating nuts.

Old trees that are large and tall, but have very little fruiting wood left inside the tree and within the base area, can be pruned back in winter so as to leave only stumps of each limb showing. The cut ends should be chamfered (see Glossary) to bark depth and a wound dressing placed on the cut surface. In hot areas it is a good idea to paint the whole stump with whitewash or a white water-based paint so as to reflect intense sunlight and prevent sunburnt limbs developing where the bark is exposed. Trees cut down like this can also be easily trained to my own pruning system if needed.

Young almond trees will grow exceedingly strongly during the first few years of establishment: it is not unusual to see new growth shoots

ALMOND BREAD

4 eggs
1 cup sugar
1 cup SR flour
1 cup plain flour
3 good handfuls of whole almonds

Using a fork, beat eggs and add sugar, then add flour and lastly add almonds. Grease and paper 2 small loaf pans. Divide mixture equally between pans and bake at 180°C for approximately 35 minutes. Remove from pans, wrap in cling wrap and freeze for a couple of days. Defrost and slice into as thin slices as possible. Place slices on ungreased baking trays or on baking paper and bake for about 6 minutes at 180°C. Don't let get too brown. Cool and store in airtight container.

grow to 2 m or more in one season. Healthy old trees that have had a severe canopy reduction also show extreme growth. Vigour within trees makes them 'throw off' (see Glossary) any young fruits that start to develop and this condition will continue until the tree settles down. One way to make the tree fruit earlier is to cincture (see Glossary) the limbs before flowering to slow down the vigour, allowing all the energy provided by the leaves to be transferred to the developing fruits. Cincturing during the spring–summer period will also make the laterals on the cinctured branch form more flower buds for the following year's crop.

Another way to slow tree growth is to train the tree to an espalier shape, making sure limbs are tied down into a horizontal or near-horizontal position, which is conducive to flower bud formation. At the same time, minimal pruning, in other words not pruning, will also promote flower bud formation (traditional espalier spur pruning systems recommend pruning all shoots as they develop to shorten growth and allow more light into trees). Non-pruning allows all shoots to grow and produce flower buds which, hopefully, will flower and set fruit in the following season, thus slowing down total plant growth.

Because the almond is the first of all the stone fruits to flower (others in this group include plums, apricots, peaches, nectarines, prunes), it is susceptible to frost from midwinter to early spring. I have seen almond trees flower as early as the first week of June in Melbourne, Victoria, where the inner city climate is very mild. Severe frosts will kill flowers and make them wilt so that they are unable to attract bees for pollination. This can in some cases lead to crop failure.

Propagation

Almonds are usually propagated by budding onto almond or peach seedlings as rootstocks. Recent developments have seen hybrid peach–almond rootstocks being trialled, but many still use 'Nemaguard', a peach seedling, as the main commercial rootstock as it is resistant to nematodes (see Glossary). It is, though, intolerant of alkaline soils, so for such soils other rootstocks should be used. Research is being done to clone by tissue culture all known successful rootstocks.

The almond is in the same family as peaches, nectarines, plums, apricots and prunes and it is possible for keen gardeners to create a multi-grafted tree containing all these fruits. However, different rootstocks will have varying success rates for different grafts. The almond is not usually budded onto apricots; although the grafts 'take' and grow, they develop large callousing 'overgrowth' at the graft union indicating an incomplete graft that will eventually fail. For more detailed coverage of grafting techniques see pp. 69–91.

Pests and diseases

There are several major pests and diseases that attack almond trees. These can be kept in check with organic or chemical sprays.

Bacterial gummosis: This disease attacks all stone fruits including almonds and shows when limbs suddenly wilt as if lacking water. If this occurs, the affected limb should be cut off well below where the infection is evident. Prune with saw or secateurs but sterilise pruning equipment in bleach or a 10% solution of methylated spirits mixed with water to prevent transferring the disease to other plants. Bacterial gummosis infection can also show as globs of sap oozing from the limbs. If the whole tree trunk or all limbs show the weeping sap then the best option is to pull out the tree as the condition will only get worse.

Shothole: This fungal disease is named shothole because of its effect on the leaves: small brown patches develop then die and fall out of the leaf leaving round holes. Fruits have gummy globules and the husk gets stuck to the nut and some twigs may die. The effect is so spectacular that it looks as if someone has fired a shotgun at the tree and riddled the leaves with lead pellets.

Close up of almond (*Prunus dulcis*) nuts in husk. Some shothole disease evident

A disease that has similar effects to gummosis and shothole is almond anthracnose.

Rust: There are many different forms of rust that infect various species of plants. The rust infecting almonds is the same that can infect other stone fruit particularly peaches, prunes and plums. It creates triangular shaped brown–yellow patches on the upper surface of leaves and shows as tiny clumps of reddish powder-like material (spores) on the underside. The disease takes its name from its appearance, particularly on leaves. It looks like rust and the powder-like 'dust' — the spores — can be rubbed off the under-surface of the leaf. Rust spores are blown about by wind or transferred in water or raindrops. Control can be initiated by using sulphur sprays, by pruning out infected sections and improving tree health. The application of liquid seaweed products to the leaf surface may indirectly help control the disease.

Rust disease on almond leaf (*Prunus dulcis*)

Aphids: These tiny insects can easily be seen with the naked eye, and can be present in large numbers on soft, growing shoots or leaves. They suck the sap from the plant and can cause leaves to grow into curled, distorted shapes. Aphids lay their eggs on plants in late autumn and it's at this stage that control measures can be initiated. Soapy water or a mineral oil spray applied while the tree is dormant will kill eggs. Once the insect has hatched the application of organic sprays such as pyrethrum is effective.

Bryobia mites: These are not true insects but are often classified by home gardeners as insect pests or spider mites because of the fact that several mite species create a fine webbing when present in large numbers and the mites do look like minute spiders when crawling on the webbing. They are hard to see with the naked eye but can easily be seen with a hand-held viewing lens. The mites do tend to build up in numbers where chemical pest and disease control measures are practised: this kills off most of the predators that naturally feed on them. A winter oil spray will kill mite eggs and the application of sulphur sprays will kill adults. It may be worthwhile trying fine sprays of mixed materials that include garlic, pyrethrum and chilli as a control measure.

Lesser insects: There are a few other insects that infest almonds at various times. Among these are San José scale that creates circular 'cone'-shaped structures on leaves, bark and fruits. When these scale are present on most fruits they cause a reddish ring to develop around the infection site. The build-up of this insect can seriously damage tree health. It is a proclaimed insect pest in some states of Australia so that spraying is mandatory. Applications of oil in winter and again in spring will help with control.

The Oriental fruit moth larvae sometimes cause damage to young shoots. The grub bores down inside the stem, eating the soft pith within, which firstly causes the shoot tip to wilt then turn black. To use a non-chemical method of control involves cutting off the still green wilted shoots well below the end of the wilted part and destroying the harvested tips. The grub will still be inside the stem of the cut shoots at this stage.

Harvesting and use of nuts

There are two distinct types of nuts produced by almonds: sweet culti-vars that give sweet kernels and bitter almonds that have nuts that taste slightly to very bitter.

Bitter almonds have hydrogen cyanide in the flesh or the meaty part of the nut. Although this substance is poisonous a person would have to consume an impossible amount to be affected. After harvesting, the skin of bitter almonds is removed allowing the creamy-white 'meaty' part of the nut to be processed. A non-drying oil is produced from bitter almonds which has been used as a sedative and in cough medicine. Prussic acid is derived from a glucoside in the kernels of bitter almonds.

Several distinct sweet nut cultivars have been selected by horticul-turists over the years and among them are very thin paper-shelled nuts that are easily broken open by hand, semi-hard shelled nuts that are not as easy to shell and very hard nuts that require placing in a nut cracker to remove the shell.

Nuts are usually harvested at the end of the summer period. Nut maturity is easily recognised because the outside husk starts to split. The husk eventually dries and separates from the nut which falls from the tree. However, the rate of fallen nuts is sporadic due to the strength of each nut's stem. Nuts slightly effected by shothole disease have gummed husks that refuse to separate from the nut so that growers usually harvest by force.

I remember working on a mixed fruit orchard and harvesting almonds by spreading hessian bags sewn together into matting. Two halves were placed around the tree to give full ground cover; then we used bamboo poles to knock branches to dislodge the nuts. They were then gathered,

CHICKEN AND ALMONDS

4 chicken breasts, skin removed
1 tbsp cornflour
1 egg white
2 tbsp sherry
Oil for frying
Mix of green and leafy vegetables,
e.g. beans, celery, broccoli, washed
and sliced
2 or 3 shallots finely sliced
1 red capsicum finely sliced
125 g toasted almonds

For sauce:
1 tbsp soy sauce
1 tbsp cornflour
1/2 cup chicken stock
Heat together and stir until thickened.

Cut chicken breasts into bite-sized
pieces. Mix in bowl with sherry,
cornflour, egg white. Quickly fry
chicken pieces in shallow pan in hot
oil until light golden, and drain well.
Heat small amount of extra oil in large
wok and saute vegetables until just
tender. Add capsicum and shallots
and stir a minute more. Add chicken
and hot sauce and top with almonds.
Serve with rice.

de-husked and let dry for a period before packaging into bags for sale to distributors. Today commercial growers use mechanical shakers to shake the trees and the nuts are gathered in large conveyor-type belts and funnelled to bins; alternatively the nuts are shaken onto the ground and a vacuum-like machine sucks them up, removing dust and rubbish, including husks. The nuts are then ready for further sorting, drying, bleaching or packaging.

Almonds should be stored in a cool, dry place and not with other fruit or vegetable products because the nuts may absorb their flavours. It is also important to protect the nuts from rodents and insects.

The almond tree is one of the few plants that, over time, has shown itself capable of surviving drought and famine, so it was a valuable food source during such times of stress. In the Mediterranean area, the place of the nut's origin, the use of almonds was noted by the early Romans. Earlier even than that, however, in the 5th century BC, almonds are mentioned in part 1 chapter 4 of *The Precious Book of Enrichment*, by Feng-Li, a Chinese diplomat writing under the nom de plume of Pao Choo Kon.

Almonds contain magnesium, phosphorous, calcium, potassium, sodium, iron, copper, manganese, folic acid, fats, protein, essential amino acids and carbohydrates. Almonds are one of the best food sources of vitamin E and supply the essential vitamin B group, especially vitamin B3.

Almonds once dried can be kept for a long time, eaten fresh, or stored and used for confectionery or decorating cakes. They can be used to make almond paste, and almond butter. One of the products made from skinned almond kernels is the popular 'marzipan' which is often moulded into shapes, coated with chocolate and sold in the chocolate trade, or used for creating layered icing on cakes, such as wedding cakes.

Oil can be extracted from the kernels and used in cooking and for flavouring alcoholic drinks. Almond oil has been prized in French cooking over centuries. It is highly perishable so needs to be stored carefully. The oil is high in oleic acid which is very easily digested and increases the absorption of fat-soluble vitamins in the daily intake. The oil contained in a handful of almonds eaten every day is reputed to improve mental concentration as well as to protect heart muscles from stress. The oil is also highly valued for use in facial creams and beauty treatments, as it is claimed to prevent wrinkles and to promote healthy glowing skin.

Immature nuts are sometimes harvested before the shell splits and before the nut becomes hardened within the developing fruit. At this stage the whole shell nut and kernel can be cut into slices and used. Another method is to pick the almond just before the kernel becomes brown. These white kernels are sliced, sometimes baked, and used for various purposes including cake decoration. I remember as a child picking green nuts from self-sown almond trees beside a road and eating the green skin of the almond before it began to dry. The taste is quite pleasant but not very sweet.

Cultivars

Early publications listing almond cultivars show most of the named cultivars still grown today. The WA Department of Agriculture's *Handbook of Horticulture and Viticulture of Western Australia* (1921) lists IXL, 'Languedoc', 'Nonpareil', 'Lauder'(seedling), 'Sanderson's Seedling' and 'Ne-Plus-Ultra'.

The 1937–1938 catalogue of C.A. Nobelius & Sons, Nurserymen of Gembrook Victoria, mentions the following cultivars: 'Brandes Jordan', 'Burbank', 'Chellaston', 'Drake's Seedling', 'Grosse Tendre', 'Harriott's Seedling', 'Hatch's Nonpareil', 'IXL', 'Johnston's Prolific', 'Ne- Plus-Ultra', 'Paper Shell', 'Peerless' and 'White Nonpareil'.

Cultivars sold in Australia today include most of the old ones plus a few new introductions: 'All-In-One', 'Brandes Jordan', 'Carmel', 'Chellaston', 'Fritz', 'Hatch's Nonpareil', 'IXL', 'Johnston's Prolific', 'Mission', 'Ne-Plus-Ultra', 'Somerton', 'Strout's Papershell' and 'Fugenso'. In America some dwarf hybrids have been developed; these may become available in Australia at some future date and would enable home gardeners to grow almonds in smaller spaces. Almond breeding work funded by various organisations such as the Horticultural Research and Development Corporation (HDRC) and government agencies, and assisted by money from the almond levy on producers, is being used to do new breeding work, evaluate cloning by tissue culture and for gene mapping (genetically identifying each cultivar) at the Waite campus of the University of Adelaide.

Brazil nuts

B e r t h o l l e t i a   e x c e l s a

The brazil nut, one of the largest nuts of all, belongs to the plant family *Lecythidaceae*, which has only two species. It is a very long-lived tree, reputed to survive to over 500 years, and is a tree of the rainforest of the Amazon Basin. It grows to 30 m or more, sometimes to 50 m.

The brazil nut is also known as the para nut and cream nut in English and has similar local names from which the English names were taken. Brazil nuts were first referred to in Western history in 1569 by the Spanish in South America. They were first imported into Europe by Dutch traders in the 17th century.

The alternate leaves of this tree are oblong or a 'boat-like' shape to about 0.5 m in length and are of a leathery texture with wavy edges to them.

The flowers are an off-white colour and the fruits that develop are huge, rounded and sometimes horny. The fruit capsule can be up to 15 cm or more in diameter and weigh up to 2.5 kg. The fruit has a very hard outer casing and when split open has some layers of pithy substance not unlike the coconut's copra to look at. Inside this layer is a pile of segmented seeds (brazil nuts) which have a very hard seed coat. The seeds have a triangular cross section and are roughly banana-shaped. There may be up to 25 of these individual seeds in the one fruit capsule and 200 or more capsules per mature tree. However, the trees may take 10–20 years or more to start producing. The nuts sometimes take up to 18 months to mature and are hand harvested when the large round fruits containing the nuts fall from the trees.

Brazil nuts are produced mostly in Brazil, Bolivia and Peru in South America. There is a huge trade in brazil nuts to the rest of the world and they are becoming more popular as people seek healthy diet regimes.

Care and maintenance

Because of propagation and pollination difficulties (see below), along with the long period before cropping begins and the need for hand harvesting, this nut is not usually grown as a plantation crop. Brazil nuts are grown mainly in natural forest conditions and managed under traditional agroforestry regimes.

The plants require relatively hot humid conditions with a high rainfall so are best suited to tropical rainforest areas of the world.

Propagation

Plants are germinated from seed and transplanted to forest plantations. Unshelled seeds can take as long as three years to germinate although the germination process can be hastened by shelling the seed. Natural propagation in the rainforest is helped by two species of rat- or squirrel-like native animals (Agoutis) that have sharp enough teeth to gnaw through the tough capsule shell and thus help spread the seed around the forest. The tree also requires the services of a native bee for pollination to occur and this bee does not survive outside its native habitat.

Brazil nut trees can be grown from seed outside their habitat area but may not produce any fruits.

There is some research being carried out into grafting as a method of propagation. Plants can also be grown by marcotting, a form of aerial layering (see Glossary).

Pests and diseases

In their forest habitat brazil nut fruit are susceptible to damage by agoutis, local insects and local fungi. Proper drying and storage are important to reduce the incidence of aflatoxin-producing fungi. Undesirably high levels of aflatoxins in food can result in aflatoxin poisoning or aflatoxicosis (see Glossary). Brazil nuts, pistachios, walnuts and pecans are susceptible to aflatoxin contamination.

Harvesting and use of nuts

The fruit of the brazil nut tree is collected regularly by hand as they fall, usually between November and August. This can be dangerous as the fruit are heavy (between 0.5 and 0.75kg each) and can fall from as high

TOFFEE BRAZIL NUTS

Blanched brazil nuts
500 g sugar
1/2 cup water
1/4 level tsp cream of tartar
1 tsp vinegar

Cover baking tray with baking paper and arrange nuts on paper with a good space around them. In a saucepan, stir sugar, water, vinegar and cream of tartar until the sugar has dissolved, then boil without stirring until the mixture is a golden honey colour. Wait until bubbles subside and the mixture has cooled slightly, then pour toffee over each nut, teaspoonful by teaspoonful. Cool. When completely cold and the toffee set remove the nuts from the paper and store in airtight jars.

This recipe can also be used for almonds or pecans.

Leathery, wavy-edged leaves

Brazilnut

single Brazil nut

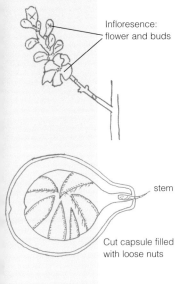

Infloresence:
flower and buds

stem

Cut capsule filled
with loose nuts

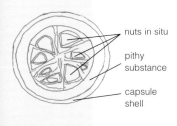

nuts in situ

pithy
substance

capsule
shell

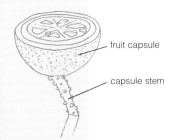

fruit capsule

capsule stem

as 50 m up the tree. The fruit are initially split, washed and dried in situ to remove some of the high moisture content, then dried further and marketed either in their shells or shelled. Brazil nuts imported into countries such as the US and Australia are subject to strict quality controls and aflatoxin checks.

Brazil nuts are high in calories, carbohydrates, protein (14%), fats, calcium, phosphorous, potassium, sodium, iron, magnesium, copper, manganese, zinc, Vitamin C, Vitamin E, Vitamins B1, B2, B3, B5, B6 and folic acid.

Brazil nuts are extremely high in selenium as they grow in selenium-rich soils. Selenium is present only in small amounts in some foods but brazil nuts have 2500 times more selenium than any other nut. Selenium is an anti-oxidant essential in human nutrition and is now known to be significant in protection against heart disease and some cancers, including prostate cancer. Selenium is also supposed to be important in discouraging the effects of aging and in stimulating the immune system.

Brazil nuts are one of the oiliest of nuts (approximately 65% digestible fat or oil) and can quite quickly go rancid. Therefore they need careful storing. Brazil nut oil can be used for salads, and as a constituent in shampoos, skin moisturisers and soaps. The seedcake remaining after oil extraction can be used for stock food.

Brazil nuts are sold in the shell or shelled, shelled and salted, raw or roasted. They are a traditional Christmas nut in Western cultures. When they were less readily available, I can remember my family having to go searching for them prior to Christmas as my grandmother so loved brazil nuts that she thought Christmas wasn't Christmas without them. Brazil nuts were then and remain a relatively expensive nut. World production has been decreasing steadily, the destruction of rainforests in South America being the main contributing factor.

Brazil nuts are also used in icecream manufacture and many confectionery products. Because they are very large nuts they often need chopping or slivering before use. They can be frozen.

The bark of the brazil nut tree has been used locally to caulk holes in boats and canoes and medicinally for liver problems. The hollowed seed pods make useful containers such as drinking cups.

Cashew nuts

Anacardium occidentale

ashew nuts (family *Anacardiaceae*) are produced on an evergreen tropical tree that can grow up to 30 m or more. This is a tree for the tropics, particularly suitable for warm areas such as Northern Queensland and the Northern Territory.

Care and maintenance

Cashew nut trees tolerate a range of soil conditions fairly well, will grow in poor soils and can get by with little maintenance. They are very drought tolerant but do require moisture during the flowering to fruiting period to maximise cropping. Drainage is important to maintain healthy trees and when grown on sandy or poor soils they should be given fertiliser as soon as they are planted and this must be continued and increased as the trees mature. The chosen fertiliser should contain all the major nutrients particularly nitrogen (N), phosphorous (P), and potassium (K); ideally all the trace elements, especially zinc and copper, should be included. Application rates will depend on the nutrient status of the soil so obtaining a soil analysis before planting is a wise move. Good organic fertilisers are an option for those using organic gardening and farming methods.

Most cashew cultivars grow into largish trees and may grow too tall to manage easily. Pruning trees at an early stage will help develop smaller, multi-branched trees. Cashew trees respond well to pruning and large specimens can be pruned very hard to keep their profile low. I have seen cashew trees in Bali virtually pruned back to high stumps and still producing many nuts

Propagation

Cashew nut trees grown commercially in places such as India, Africa and South East Asia are commonly produced from seed. Trees propagated by this method may vary significantly in their growth habit and shape as well as in the quality and size of the nuts and the amount produced per tree. When the shells are removed the nuts may be very small, weighing as little as 2 g, or they may weigh 30 g or more.

Selected cultivars of cashews are better propagated by budding, using the shield budding method, as this is found to be the most reliable.

In Australia the CSIRO, other government departments and private companies have set up plantations and are experimenting with growing cultivars of cashew nuts in selected places on different soil types to assess how they perform under Australian conditions. There are plantations in Queensland and the Northern Territory, amongst other places.

Cashew nut tree (*Anacardium occidentale*) foliage, with old flower debris and nuts forming, showing the 'cashew apple' near ripe

Some 5000 cultivars were developed by the CSIRO between 1988 and 1992 and from these it is likely that a number of superior quality cultivars will eventually emerge. Some of the CSIRO selections are for bushy growth trees and when these become available, many problems of size will be alleviated, as well as the necessity for pruning.

Pests and diseases

Although cashew nut trees do not suffer from many pests or diseases, trees should be regularly checked. A few Australian native insects such the mango tip borer (*Pencillaria jocosatrix*), the giant termite (*Mastotermes dawinensis*) and the fruit spotting bug (*Amblypelta lutescens*) do attack the trees and can cause minor problems. Flying foxes have been known to eat the cashew 'apple' but drop the nut section.

CASHEW NUT BUTTER

Grind or process a quantity of cashew nuts (about two cups) to a paste and then gradually add melted butter or light oil (1/4 cup or a bit more), mixing the whole time, until a buttery consistency is achieved. Transfer to a butter dish and store in refrigerator until needed. Can be used in sandwiches or on biscuits. Note that this butter can also be flavoured with vinegar or lemon juice to result in a cashew nut mayonnaise. Other nuts such as macadamia, toasted almonds, or hazelnuts can also be used in this way.

Cashew nuts (*Anacardium occidentale*) with 'cashew apple' still attached

Harvesting and use of nuts

The cashew nuts that we eat are actually seeds (kernel) of the plant. The way the fruit is formed and the seed produced is unique, and very interesting. The clusters (panicles) of yellow–pink cashew flowers are followed by fruits bearing the nuts at their basal end.

A cashew fruit, called the cashew 'apple', is very high in vitamin C content. It is formed from the swollen, enlarged and elongated flower stem and can be coloured reddish, pink or yellowish. It is soft-textured and can be eaten raw and is often used to produce sweet things such as jam, syrup, sweetmeats and wine. At the end of the cashew 'apple' is the kidney-shaped cashew nut enclosed in a hard, thick, tight-fitting porous skin (husk). Under the shell is a layer of material producing a dark-coloured acrid, corrosive oil containing a chemical called cardol. This material is also present in the sap and is similar to that produced by the poison ivy (*Toxicodendron radicans*) which is in the same plant family (*Anacardiaceae*) as the cashew nut. It causes skin allergies and other damage to sensitive skins. The cashew shell nut liquid (CSNL) is incorporated into patented products such as special corrosion-resistant paints, insulation products and brake linings. The nuts we eat are roasted to get rid of these poisonous oils. When handling unroasted cashews it is essential to wear protective gloves to avoid injury.

All cashews sold for eating have been toasted, shelled and then heat treated to remove the cardol, even the ones sold as 'raw'. Australian produced nuts are usually processed in China or India as the manual labour needed is costly in Australia. The edible kernel (nut) can be eaten raw or in the most readily available form: roasted, salted or unsalted to taste. There has been a recent growth in 'add on' products including cashew nuts covered in chocolate or honey to sell to various markets.

Cashew nuts provide lipids and protein and have a greater concentration of essential amino acids than many other nuts. Also available from cashew nuts are carbohydrates, calcium, phosphorous, potassium, sodium, iron, magnesium, zinc and vitamin A, vitamins B1,B2,B3, B5, and folic acid. Cashews contain less fat than other nuts and can therefore be stored much longer.

Chestnuts

Castanea spp.

This is a diverse group of deciduous species originating from various parts of the world and including some that are grown for food. They belong to the *Fagaceae* family and include the Spanish (or European) chestnut (*Castanea sativa*), Chinese chestnut (*Castanea mollisima*), Japanese chestnut (*Castanea crenata*) and the American chestnut (*Castanea dentata*). European chestnuts are larger and not as sweet as American chestnuts. Chinese chestnuts are smaller and Japanese chestnuts vary in size. Neither is as sweet as the American chestnut.

Chestnut cultivars grown in Australia are *C. sativa* selections and include 'April Gold', 'Buffalo Queen', 'Fleming Beauty', 'Knox Early', 'Oregon Barcelona', 'Purton's Pride', 'Red Spanish', 'Sassafras Red', 'Sword' and 'Wandiligong Wonder'. Quarantine laws prevent other chestnut species being imported into Australia because of the fear of introducing pests and diseases, in particular chestnut blight which could kill all trees already planted.

Chestnuts are usually grown in cool mountain areas with high rainfall. They are slightly drought tolerant when established but cannot withstand water logging, which is likely to make them susceptible to root rots. Chestnuts make excellent shade trees in summer months and produce glowing colours during autumn. I have seen chestnuts grown as street trees in Heathcote in Victoria and they make a fine specimen tree with their dark green foliage of deeply serrated leaves.

Chestnuts have been grown in Australia for about 150 years, but interest in planting large commercial groves did not occur until the 1970s. In Australia, commercial chestnuts are grown around Manjimup (WA), in the Adelaide Hills (SA), the Dandenong Ranges near Melbourne, North Eastern Victoria near Wangaratta, Batlow and Orange (NSW) and in Tasmania.

Sweet chestnut (*Castanea sativa*) tree grown as a street tree, Heathcote, Victoria

Sweet chestnuts (*Castanea sativa*) ready for roasting

Care and maintenance

Chestnut trees can eventually grow to a huge size, up to 20 m, when planted in their preferred rich well-drained soils so they are not well suited to small home gardens. When they become too large chestnut trees can be pruned lightly or severely and will recover easily.

Commercial growers usually train trees to a central leader (pyramid shape) system but many have started pruning the centre out of the central leader system (creating a delayed vase shape) to open trees and reduce tree size.

Chestnuts are deep-rooted plants that can crop well year after year without much fertiliser, but growers usually give a handful of some complete fertiliser just after planting and gradually increase this amount as the tree ages.

ROASTED CHESTNUTS

Chestnuts are delicious roasted and this can easily be done in the oven or in a pan on top of the stove. Using a sharp knife make 2 deep crosswise cuts on the flat side of the shell. Coat the chestnuts lightly with oil. If roasting, place in a single layer on a baking tray covered with baking paper and roast at 180–200°C for approximately 30 minutes or until shells come away easily. For a pan method, place chestnuts in a single layer in a pre-heated heavy-based pan or skillet and cook over medium to high heat until shells come away easily. The shells and inner skin should be removed as soon as the chestnuts are cool enough.

Propagation

Chestnut trees are easily grafted and the use of a whip and tongue graft to place scions onto seedling-grown trees is a popular method (see pp. 71–85 on grafting); this is usually done in early spring. Older trees can also be regrafted to better cultivars by 'pollarding' trees to a basic stump framework and grafting these limbs in spring using cleft and bark grafts.

Pests and diseases

There are many severely debilitating pests and diseases of chestnuts, such as chestnut blight caused by the fungus (*Endothia parasitica*), which have killed most of the American chestnut trees (*Castanea dentata*) and has meant that the American chestnut industry is no longer commercially viable. They are not recorded in this country and thanks to strict quarantine regulations should be kept at bay.

Root rot caused by *Phytopthora cinnamomi* is a fungus that troubles chestnuts and is a disease that cannot be easily controlled. It is wise to remove the whole tree and all the root system of infected trees to curtail the spread of this disease.

Phomopsis sp. (nut rot) is the major post-harvest disease to threaten chestnut growers as the infected nuts are made unpalatable by the bitter taste that develops in the kernel, which will eventually soften then rot.

European chestnut
(*Castanea sativa*)
flower head,
December 1992

European chestnut
(*Castanea sativa*)
splitting husks and
seed, April 1992

Trials are being carried out to determine whether rot-resistant cultivars are among those now available in Australia and to discover whether methods such as hot water dips before storage can prevent infection occurring. Weevils can also be a problem during post-harvest storage.

Birds such as cockatoos and parrots may attack the nuts as they mature, and cause some losses.

Harvesting and use of nuts

Chestnuts are harvested when they fall from the trees. The nuts are enclosed in a very prickly, hairy husk and it is wise to use gloves when handling them. They can be separated from the husk and then stored in a cool refrigerator. Cool storage is needed because the nuts have a high respiration rate and need high humidity to reduce this in order to store well. In other words, the nuts would otherwise dry out quickly and not be as satisfactory for eating.

Chestnuts have to be cooked and shelled before they are added to other food. They can be boiled but are usually roasted. In the northern hemisphere roasted chestnuts are a feature of autumn. Chestnut vendors are a very common sight in the streets and market places and at festivals in Europe but this is rare in Australia. In China during the chestnut season street vendors are commonly seen roasting fresh chestnuts on a coal-fired brazier.

Nuts can be peeled, and some research into peeled frozen chestnuts is being trialled to extend the life of the nuts and to create other delectable chestnut products. There are also many new 'add on' approaches including chocolate-coated or toffee-covered nuts. The kernels can be used in cakes, flour, jams, and biscuits. Sweetened chestnut puree is used in cakes and pastry fillings. In Britain, chestnuts have been used as a traditional stuffing for roasted turkeys and other poultry at Christmas, and in France, *marron glacé*, chestnuts preserved in syrup, is a popular delicacy.

Chestnuts (*Castanea sativa*) contain dietary fibre, potassium, protein, fats, oils, amino acids, carbohydrates, calcium, phosphorous, sodium, iron, magnesium, zinc, copper, manganese,vitamin C, vitamin E, vitamins B 1, B2, B3, B5,and B6. They have a very low fat content compared to other tree nuts and are very low in calories.

Coconuts

Cocos nucifera

The coconut palm (family *Palmae*) is a truly tropical plant preferring coastal regions and tropical island beaches. Its origin is difficult to determine but it is thought to come from Asia or Polynesia. The palm tree has a bare trunk and a central growing apex with fern-like fronds up to 7 m long. These palms can, under ideal conditions, reach a height of 30 m or more, making harvesting difficult as it is usually done by hand. One mature palm tree can produce up to 400 coconuts which can take up to one year to mature. The coconut is inside a large, rounded husk, which prevents the nut smashing to pieces when it falls from the tree at maturity.

There are several different forms (cultivars) of this species, including some with a tall growth habit and some dwarf plants that produce smaller golden (or orange or yellow) husked coconuts and golden-stemmed fronds.

Coconut oil, desiccated coconut (copra), shredded coconut, coconut milk, coconut cream, raw juice and raw copra are used constantly by cooks and by some as an everyday food item. Consequently myriad delicious recipes have been devised. Coconut milk and coconut cream are often added to other food items to enhance their flavour.

EASY COCONUT MACAROONS

1 can sweetened condensed milk
1 packet desiccated coconut

Mix together and place in spoonfuls on a greased baking tray and bake until turning golden brown on peaks. Remove from tray when cool.

Care and maintenance

Coconut palms need well-drained sandy soil and can flourish with some saline water influx around their root system. They can grow in other soil types away from coastal areas but may not fruit. Palms can manage with natural rainfall, but young plants should be watered during dry periods or when grown in pots.

There is no real need to prune coconut palm trees: they lose their old fronds naturally as they grow upwards. Sometimes, however, the leaves are pruned as soon as they become tattered and are in decline. Pruning the top growth point out of the coconut palm will kill the plant. Coconut palms tend to grow crookedly or with a bent trunk in the natural environment so staking the plant in its early growth years may be an option if a straight trunk is needed.

Some organic fertiliser will help promote growth, and protection from tropical cyclonic winds may be necessary while the palms are young and have not yet developed an anchoring root system. There are no major pests or diseases that trouble this plant.

Coconut palm
(*Cocos nucifera*)
trees near beach

Yellow fruited
coconut palm
(*Cocos nucifera*),
Cairns, Qld

Propagation

This tropical plant is easily grown from seed; in fact a dehusked coconut placed on damp sandy soil in a shady place in the humid tropics will self-germinate without any aid within 1–4 months. The shoot appears first so that a coconut seems to be growing without roots, but is using the stored food and liquid 'milk' within the coconut to get started. At this stage it should be planted to ensure the seedling's survival.

Coconuts have been known to float for hundreds of kilometres by sea to be dumped upon beaches and it is thought that the predominance of coconut trees on some small Pacific islands and atolls is because the species has spread by this method.

Common problems

While no major pests or diseases threaten coconut palm trees in Australia, bud rot, some caterpillars, grasshoppers, scale and a tree-trunk borer have been found attacking plants.

Harvesting and use

The coconut is probably one of the most valuable plants known because of its multiple uses, as food, timber, artifacts and many others. Some Pacific Islanders rely on the coconut as a staple food item. The white coconut meat (copra), the nut, shell and husk, as well as the leaves and trunk of the palm, provide an enormous range of products. Palm leaves are made into thatch or matting and used for roofing, and the fronds can even be used for clothing; leaf stems with leaflets removed are used as poles and spikes; the wood is used for buildings and for carving.

The coconut provides a fermented wine brewed from the flower stalks. The spent coconut shell can be used as a drinking container, and

LUMBERJACK CAKE

2 medium apples	1 cup sugar	1/2 cup brown sugar
500 g dates	1 egg	(well packed in)
1 tsp bi-carbonate soda	1 tsp vanilla	1/3 cup milk
1 cup boiling water	1 1/2 cups plain flour	1 cup shredded coconut
125 g butter	60 g butter	

Peel, core and chop apples. Combine with chopped dates, bi-carb and boiling water and set aside until lukewarm. Cream butter and sugar, add egg and vanilla and beat well. Add flour alternately with fruit mix. Pour into greased and lined 20 cm spring form tin and bake 70 minutes in moderate oven.

Combine extra butter, brown sugar, milk and shredded cocnut in small saucepan and stir over low heat until butter and sugar have melted. Spread over hot cake and bake further 2 minutes until topping golden brown.

for making utensils. The outer fibrous husk is used for packaging and producing coconut fibre mats or rope. Waste coconut material from processing is recycled into compressed 'bricks' as 'copra peat' or 'palm peat' and is used in the plant nursery industry and in home gardens as a potting mix or as a medium for propagating plants.

Coconuts can be harvested by hand or with long cutters, or by using machines such as cherry pickers to reach tall plants. The coconuts take over one year to reach maturity. Alternatively the nuts can be harvested as they fall to the ground but fallen coconuts are often regarded as being of poorer quality compared to those cut from the palm tree. A dehusked coconut will store for several months. While the shell is still soft, young immature nuts are harvested for their meat (copra) as well as the coconut milk contained within. Immature coconuts are sliced open at one end to get to the coconut milk and the husk/soft nut shells are used as drinking containers.

With hard-shelled mature coconuts the outer husk is peeled away and holes punched into the nut, usually at the place where the three 'eyes' (pores) are — the shell is less dense at these points — to extract the milk, or the coconut is cracked open to obtain the copra. This can be eaten raw, dried, or shredded and soaked in water to extract coconut 'cream' to be used for many cooking purposes and for drinks. The main central growth shoot is sometimes harvested and used as a vegetable, but its removal actually kills the palm tree.

Copra is an important source of oil for culinary and industrial purposes. It is used commercially for soap, for margarine and, because of its good keeping qualities, in many prepared and packaged foods.

Coconuts provide many calories and have carbohydrates, protein, fat, oils, calcium, phosphorous, potassium, sodium, iron, magnesium, copper, manganese, vitamin C, vitamin E, and small amounts of vitamins B1, B2, B3, B5, B6 and some folic acid.

Coconut palm (*Cocos nucifera*), coconuts and palm leaves, Bali, 1996

Cultivars

There are several seedling selections including those that produce coloured fruits. Some dwarf cultivars, such as 'Dwarf Fijian' and 'Dwarf Malaysian', are also available. There are no commercial plantations in Australia although plants (grown from seed) are commonly seen on the northern beaches and tropical islands and are planted in parks and gardens in places such as Darwin.

Hazelnuts

or filberts (cobnuts, monkey nuts)

Corylus avellana

The hazelnut is a bush or small tree commonly known as the European hazel (filbert). All the above names are also used for the common nut from the *Corylus* species (family *Betulaceae*) depending on your information sources or the country that you live in. Barcelona nut is the name given to a nut introduced from or bred in Barcelona, Spain. The term 'hazel' and 'hazelnut' usually refer to a nut that has a husk shorter than the nut. 'Cob' and 'cobnut' are other common names for the hazelnut. The word 'filbert' was originally thought to refer to nuts with a long husk or beard. The name monkey nut comes from the appearance of the nut as it has eye-like spots on the shell giving the nut a monkey-like face. These names are sometimes confused but botanists have decided on the common name 'filbert' for all *Corylus* species. It is the correct technical term, though it may take a long time for general usage of the common name hazelnut to change. Hazelnut is used generally in this publication.

Hazelnuts (filberts) include ten or so separate edible nut-producing shrub and tree species and many cultivars from several areas of the world including Europe, the Americas and Asia. Many other separate species have been previously described in literature but have recently, through chromosome testing and advanced botanical recognition methods, been found to be cultivars of other known species. The hazelnut of commerce (*C. avellana*) has a

---

HAZELNUT BISCUITS

150 g butter
150 g sugar
zest of lemon
2 egg yolks
85 g cornflour
200 g plain flour
175 g roasted hazelnuts chopped.

Cream butter and sugar. Add egg yolks and zest. Fold in flours and the nuts. Roll dough into a sausage, wrap in cling wrap and refrigerate for half an hour or so. Unwrap and cut roll into 1/2 cm wide slices. Place on greased baking tray and bake at about 180°C for about 15 minutes or until golden.

very wide natural distribution that includes most of Europe through to
Iran, Lebanon, Syria and Turkey. There are also several species and cultivars that have ornamental value only, such as those with coloured leaf
forms. The most recognisable to home gardeners is the form (C. *avellana* 'Contorta', sometimes called 'crazy filbert') that has twisted branches
that grow into angular contorted shapes.

Hazelnuts have both male and female flowers but all species are self-
infertile, that is, they need another plant or species nearby to provide
pollen to enable the plant to produce nuts. Pollen is produced by 2–4
cm catkins (male flowers). The female flowers are tiny, round, bud-like
structures with red protuberances. These trees, though, have a very con-
fusing pollination–fertilisation process which makes them very choosy
so that they will not accept just any pollen. The tree supplying pollen
must be compatible and produce it at the right time for pollination to

Hazelnut tree
(*Corylus avellana*)
in August showing
flowering

Hazelnut tree
(*Corylus avellana*
'Contorta'):
Ornamental 'Crazy
Filbert' tree with
zig- zag branches

Hazelnut tree
(*Corylus avellana*),
immature nuts on
tree showing
green husks

occur, so it is not always easy to find the right partner for a hazelnut tree.

Commercial hazelnuts are usually produced from C. *avellana*, the European hazelnut (filbert). This is the main species grown commercially because it is the one producing the largest nuts and the largest crops. Many cultivars have arisen from crossing species and by selecting seedling trees (mainly of C. *avellana*) that show promise for nut production. Every seedling that is grown from seed is actually a new cultivar even though the nuts from those trees may mirror those of the parent tree.

Many countries have grown trees of C. *avellana* from imported seed and gradually developed their nut industry from selections of the introduced material. In Australia, the trees of many established early orchards were originally grown from seed. As a consequence, some quite specific Australian selections have developed such as 'Wanliss Pride', 'Myrtleford', 'Tokolyi' and 'Altas', many of which have originated in orchards as 'chance' seedlings. Many of the nuts that were first introduced into Australia were imported as seed (nuts) and so the name given to the trees that were produced have in lots of cases not been true to the original cultivar type. To complicate matters some cultivars have over time been given more than one name, making it very hard to distinguish separate cultivars and extremely difficult to find compatible species for cross-pollination purposes.

All the naming complications aside hazelnuts or filberts have a long and interesting story going back beyond recorded history. At one of the earliest Mesolithic (7000 BC–4000 BC) sites at Mountsandel in Coleraine (Londonderry in Ireland), evidence has been found that hazelnuts formed part of the mixed diet of early modern humans. They were known in the Middle Ages in western Europe as well as in Russia where they were gathered from forests. The first recorded use of the name 'hazelnuts' goes back before the 12th century. Hazelnut trees symbolised justice for the ancient Celts as well as love and reconciliation. Hazelnuts, or filberts as they were known, were first grown in America in the 1800s.

Care and maintenance

Hazelnuts grow best in areas that have cooler humid summers with temperatures not exceeding 29°C and cold winters. These trees are intolerant of strong winds, and extreme heat and moisture stress. Areas that are ideal receive some cold weather during autumn–winter and have a dry period during the harvest months in early autumn. Many hazelnut cultivars require a quite specific number of hours of cold weather to enable them to produce good crops. Some need less than others and the recent introduction of some newer cultivars that require fewer cool hours will, if they are successful, increase the range of cultivation areas. Currently, hazelnuts grow well in many areas of Tasmania, the Central Tablelands of NSW (cultivar trials have been set up in Orange), Coastal Southern NSW (in areas such as Bega Valley), North-Eastern Victoria (especially Ovens Valley), and South-Eastern Victoria in the Gippsland region.

Hazelnuts grow in any well-drained, rich, fertile soil and seem to grow best in areas that have 700-1050 mm rainfall per year. The trees are usually planted about 3–4 m apart but can be grown in closer plantings as hedgerows or as single trees trained with a high central trunk. It is important to irrigate during the summer months particularly during nut formation in early summer. Mulching of the root area under the trees helps retain moisture.

Technically or 'botanically' the pollination of the hazelnut is an oddity as it does not follow typical pollination-fertilisation sequences that have evolved in other plants. Hazelnuts are wind pollinated; they have both the male and female flowers on the one plant but these are mostly non-self-pollinating and need a compatible pollen donor from another cultivar. There is some difficulty in finding good pollen donors for specific cultivars.

The male flower(s) is catkin form, a compressed, rounded, hanging, tubular growth containing many minute flowers. The catkin is initiated during mid-summer when the current season's nut crop is still on the tree. The female flower is initiated at a slightly later stage. By February, the catkins can easily be seen hanging from the tree laterals and tiny, enlarged, rounded 'buds' that will be the female flower are also evident. At maturity the female 'bud' develops a clump of red antennae to receive pollen. The catkins grow to about half their mature size and become dormant until winter, when they grow again and begin shedding pollen. Each individual catkin can shed millions of pollen grains although only a single grain is needed for pollination. The female flowers which contain vegetative growth buds also go through a dormancy period until the winter flowering. When pollination occurs the pollen grain initiates pollen tube growth, but this is also suspended for a time and fertilisation does not actually occur until early summer. The nuts grow to maturity during summer and fall from trees during the early autumn period.

Propagation

Propagation of hazelnuts is usually by seed or by layering or digging out suckers (from non-grafted trees). The trees tend to sucker profusely so when a hazelnut is known to produce good crops of good-sized nuts, this is a good way for home gardeners to increase orchard size. Suckers from

VEGETARIAN NUT ROAST WITH CHEESE AND TOMATOES

1 onion chopped
1 clove garlic chopped
Butter
250 g mixed nuts
150 g stale wholemeal bread
100 ml vegetable stock
Fresh or dried herbs to taste (e.g. thyme, oregano, sage, rosemary, basil)

Saute onions and garlic in butter. Put nuts and bread together in food processor and grind. Combine all ingredients into a firm mix. Put half the mixture into a greased and lined loaf pan. Cover with a layer of sliced tomatoes and a layer of parmesan or romano cheese, then top with remaining nut mixture. Bake at 180°C for about 30 minutes or until brown on top. Cool in pan, then remove and wrap in greaseproof paper and refrigerate before cutting into slices.

With a little more stock the nut mixture can also be used to make nut rissoles.

grafted trees will not come true to type but can be used as a rootstock onto which known cultivars can be grafted.

Propagation by cutting is an option but, unfortunately, cuttings taken from hazelnuts rarely root readily, with only about a 30% success rate. The cultivars that produce the best crops of nuts seem to be particularly difficult to propagate from cuttings. For best results, dormant cuttings can be placed into a well-drained loose propagation medium; the use of a root-promoting hormone such as IBA may enhance rooting percentage. Cuttings taken from growing shoots in late summer can also be used, usually with a greater success rate.

Propagation by grafting is not easy either: for hazelnuts to callus at the graft point an optimum temperature of about 27°C is needed. Various ways to overcome this have been tried, including cutting the scion wood in autumn–winter and storing it in a refrigerator at about 0°C until ready for use during

Hazelnut tree
(*Corylus avellana*),
harvested husks
and nuts in shell

Hazelnut tree
(*Corylus avellana*),
catkin infected
with mites

Hazelnut tree
(*Corylus avellana*),
leaf showing sooty
mould on surface

the warm summer months. In America, propagators use electrically heated hot caps/sleeves around the graft union for extra heat.

I have had success with my new approach to spring grafting where, as with other species, I use a hollow plastic sleeve placed over the graft and scion. The plastic 'tube' is cut from a section of packaging plastic, then sealed at the top end but left open at the base. Before inserting the sleeve over the graft, I squirt some water into the tube to provide humidity. The sleeve is placed over the graft and the base held in place with a mapping pin or ordinary sewing pin. I do this grafting in spring but it can be done at any time. However, if you do it during the hot summer period, place a paper bag over the plastic sleeve to prevent the scion being sunburnt. The plastic sleeve can be removed when new foliage growth from the inserted scion partially or fully fills the space inside the sleeve (for more detail see pp. 71–85 on grafting).

One way to produce more plants from a given tree is to practise the art of layering (see Glossary and pp. 69–91 on propagation for further information).

Pests and diseases

Hazelnuts grown in Australia rarely suffer any major pest or disease problem. This is mainly because of strict quarantine regulations on the import of plant material, which has prevented the accidental introduction of many pests and diseases that could cause serious economic losses.

Hazelnut blight which attacks leaves and causes dieback of shoots has been detected in Australia. Black sooty mould often seen on leaves is a fungus that lives on exudations of insects feeding on the leaves. Aphids are often present where sooty mould is found. They suck sap from leaves and sooty mould may grow on the juices exuded by these insects. The aphids in turn may be fed on by ladybirds which can provide some natural control.

Hazelnut buds are often infected with tiny mites including eriophyid mites that cannot be seen with the naked eye. They cause the condition known as 'big bud', a swelling of the bud to several times its normal size. This problem has not been seen to any extent in Australia although examination of buds often shows the presence of several mite species including predator mites which may be reducing the troublesome 'big bud' mite population. Hazelnut catkins sometimes become ragged and rough in appearance instead of being smooth; this can be caused by eriophyid mite infection.

Native birds such as parrots and cockatoos enjoy these nuts and fallen nuts are sometimes taken by foxes.

Harvesting and use of nuts

Hazelnuts usually fall from the tree so are easily collected. Netting or some form of matting on the ground under the tree can be used to collect the nuts but if the grass around the tree is kept well mown they are easy to see and collect. The nuts should not come into contact with soil particles which could encourage fungal rots and/or insect attack.

Hazelnuts are used extensively in European cooking, either ground or chopped. They make a delicious salad oil. The oil has also been used in cough treatments and medicines, and in perfumes. It formed an important component of paint in the nineteenth century, valued for its good drying qualities.

Hazelnuts contain fats and oils, amino acids, and compared with other nuts are one of the best suppliers of vitamin E. They also supply zinc, selenium, vitamin A, calcium and potassium, and all the basic vitamin B group are present especially B5 and B6. Hazelnuts are high in fats but do not have as much protein as some other tree nuts.

In Tasmania, there is now a move to produce traditional European truffles. Hazelnut trees root-inoculated with the truffle fungus are being grown, but to date only a few truffles have been produced.

Cultivars

Hazelnut (filbert) cultivars commonly available include:'Barcelona', 'Butler', 'Cob' ('Gunslebert'), 'Cosford' ('Coxford'),'Davianna', 'Ennis', 'Halls Giant', 'Red Avelline', 'Wanliss Pride' and 'White Avelline'.

Precise information on which cultivar will pollinate successfully with other cultivars is not readily available. The pollinators 'Butler', 'Davianna' or 'Halls Giant' seem to be compatible with most other cultivars and can be planted with or grafted onto them to improve cropping.

Until recently, hazelnut growers have been individuals, mostly with small holdings. As a result the industry has not been well co-ordinated. With recent grants from government agencies much more research is being undertaken to find the best hazelnut pollinator types and to introduce more cultivars into Australia. Although there is a very limited number of cultivars available for home gardeners at present this should change in the future as more introduced ones become available.

Some of the new cultivars being trialled and which may become available if successful include: 'American White', 'Atlas', 'Barcelona-Oregon', 'Barcelona-NE' (Myrtleford), 'Casina', 'Cosford-Turkish', 'Imperial de Tribizonde', 'Kentish Cob', 'Lambert', 'Negret', 'Oregon Barcelona', 'Royal', 'Segorbe', 'Square Sheild', 'Tokolyi' (Cosford), 'Tonda Gentile delle Langhe', 'Tonda di Giffoni', 'Tonda Romana', 'Tonollo', 'Willamette' and 'Woodnut'.

Macadamias

Macadamia integrifolia

The macadamia (family *Proteaceae*) is one of the very few fruit- or nut-producing trees of Australian origin that has been extensively developed for commercial production. Australian Aborigines used this tree as a food source for thousands of years. The explorer Leichhardt in 1843 was the first European to collect the nuts but the tree was not actually named until 1858 when rediscovered by Ferdinand von Muller who collected his own samples.

In 1909, F.M. Bailey, colonial botanist of Queensland described the macadamia in *Comprehensive Catalogue of Qeensland Plants*, and listed several new species, M. *lowii*, M. *minor*, M. *praealta*, and M. 'Wheleni'. He noted the varying forms of the plant found growing wild. Elliot and Jones in *Encyclopaedia of Australian Plants Vol. 6* describe the genus macadamia as consisting of six Australian species and of those, M. *heyana*, named by Bailey, is listed. M. *lowii* and M. *minor* have now been recognised as synonyms of M. *ternifolia* which is commonly known as the Small-fruited Bush Nut, an ideal small bushy plant for home gardens but which produces nuts with bitter tasting kernels. M. *integrifolia* and M. *tetraphylla* and cultivars of these two species are the ones grown commercially for nut production.

The trees have leaves whorled around the stem and produce clusters of large, marble-shaped fruit (nuts) with a hard, shiny, rough shell and a kernel that is delicious when roasted.

M. *integrifolia*, the Smooth-shelled Bush Nut, grows to about 10–15 m and is endemic to the south-eastern parts of Queensland. It is found in rainforest areas, often growing with M. *tetraphylla* with which it hybridises readily. The dehusked nuts of M. *integrifolia* can be up to 2 cm or more in diameter and have a very smooth, often glistening, hard, honey-brown coloured shell. This tree is bushy and has thin, whorled leaves to about 20 cm long and 3–5 cm wide, which are toothed and wavy with prickly edges.

M. *tetraphylla*, the Rough-shelled Bush Nut, occurs naturally in NSW and Queensland and grows to a size similar to M. *integrifolia*. Trees usually have four to five whorled leaves varying from 5–30 cm long and 2–5 cm wide. The leaves are very coarsely toothed with spiny edges. As with M. *integrifolia* the massed, hanging, white to pink flowers (called racemes—see Glossary) are long and bottlebrush shaped. The 2–3 cm nuts are roundish, brown in colour and have a rough or 'bubbly' surface. The spiky leaves of this species can be a problem if it is used as a garden plant.

The first commercial interest in the macadamia nut occurred, interestingly, in Hawaii where macadamia nut trees were first planted during 1892 and research work selecting cultivars began about 40 years later. Commercial interest did not really begin in Australia until the 1950s when Hawaii cultivars were imported for trial experiments. There are more trials with selected Australian seedlings and hybrids being carried out now with the aim of of producing better cultivars. There are many criteria being used to select new cultivars including the shape and fruiting habit of trees, their resistance to pests and diseases, their ability to produce larger and earlier crops and to adapt to temperature extremes. The chase is also on to find trees that produce nuts ideal for commercial processing, that have thinner shells and husks that don't adhere, are easy to crack open without harming the kernel, have a short harvest period, produce nuts of a regular shape and size with a high oil content and a recovery rate higher than the accepted norm of about 36% for high grade nuts. Home gardeners will benefit from the better selection of trees that will become available.

Commercial production of macadamias is increasing rapidly around the world with plantations now in California and Florida in the US, and in many parts of South America, Africa and South-East Asia.

Care and maintenance

Macadamia trees grow in semi-tropical areas of Australia but will grow outside that range if they are planted in well-drained soils. Home gardeners in Sydney and Melbourne regularly grow their own trees from

---

MACADAMIA NUT TART

Pie tin lined with shortcrust pastry and blind baked
500 g macadamia nuts
4 eggs
1/2 cup brown sugar
3 tbsp melted butter
3/4 cup light corn (or maple) syrup
1 tsp vanilla essence

Fill blind baked pastry shell with macadmia nuts. Beat eggs and then mix in all other ingredients. Pour over nuts. Bake at 200°C for 10 minutes then at 180° for a further 30–40 minutes until set. Serve with whipped cream flavoured with vanilla sugar.

seed with great success. Trees from seed will always grow nuts at some stage although they may take from five to eight years to crop. Some seedling cultivars produce nuts with extremely hard, thick shells so it is necessary to have a good nut-cracker handy. Macadamia nut trees will grow in the southern parts of Australia: on Bruny Island in the far south of Tasmania, I know of one tree growing quite well, although it has not yet set fruit and may not do so because the trees are susceptible to frost and extended cold periods, particularly at flowering time.

Macadamia trees can be grown organically with the help of predator insects, using approved organic practices, organic fertilisers and spray materials. To achieve good crops, the main focus should be on orchard management, tree health, fertiliser applications, pruning and weed control. Before starting to grow macadamia trees organically it is worth obtaining a soil analysis to check for any major or minor nutrient deficiencies. Larger crops are often obtained when, for instance, zinc foliar sprays are applied in areas where the soil is deficient in zinc.

Macadamia trees do not usually need pruning but can be if necessary. Some commercial producers keep the trees pruned as hedges.

Propagation

Macadamia trees have traditionally been grown from seed, but larger nutted, thinner shelled cultivars can be propagated by budding and grafting onto selected rootstocks or by taking cuttings.

Budding and grafting are used for propagation because not all sown seed will germinate (see pp. 71–85 on grafting). The first attempts to bud and graft macadamia species using traditional methods was a relative failure as only a 30% success rate was achieved. Some cultivars that are difficult to graft still have very low success rates. Experimenting with preparation of budwood material and the use of an oval-shaped patch budding system improved success rates.

Budding and grafting techniques are used by nurseries to enable large-scale reproduction. Some macadamia propagators take cuttings but most trees are grafted. Seed grafting is also used. The germinating seedling has its soft shoot removed and the short stem that remains is cut downwards forming a cleft and is grafted using tiny scion shoots. Air layering can also produce new plants.

M. *tetraphylla* selections are the preferred rootstocks for grafting macadamia trees but trials are under way to assess others. Rootstock seed is germinated in trays or beds and the young plants transplanted into pots and kept under partial shade. The rootstocks are grown for about 18 months to obtain a good-sized trunk before budding or grafting in early autumn or early spring. The scion wood can be prepared by making sure

Small grafted
macadamia nut
tree (*Macadamia
integrifolia*), Narre
Warren, Victoria

Handful of
macadamia nuts
(*Macadamia
integrifolia*) from
seedling tree,
Melbourne, Victoria

the plants are healthy and by cincturing the limbs that are going to be used as scion material. This cincturing allows food produced by the leaves to stay in the scion shoot which is removed after a few weeks, cut and prepared for grafting or budding.

The grafts that have been used on macadamias include whip grafts, side-wedge grafts, and bark grafts for larger limbs or reworked trees. Patch budding has been used with great success in Queensland. The rootstock material and the scion donor trees are given food and water a few weeks before the budwood is taken and the rootstocks grafted to increase sap flow.

Rootstocks are prepared by making sure the condition of the bark is ideal and that it 'slips' easily. A small hollow or oval tubular implement with sharp edges can be used to cut the bud from the scion. The leaves are cut from the donor wood to leave a short leaf stalk. The implement is placed over the bud and leaf stalk and pressed into the bark, then given a slight twist. If the bark is at the correct stage the oval bark piece including a bud will detach from the budstick. The implement is then used to create another oval patch anywhere on the rootstock stem and the bud patch transferred to this. Because the patches are identical in size and shape this method results in a perfect match at the bark edge and increases percentage take. The patch is covered with budding tape leaving the bud exposed or it can be fully covered as an option.

Pests and diseases

There are several native insects that have adapted to the macadamia and trees are at times attacked by many more. There are, however, only a few species that can cause problems. These are the fruit spotting bug, macadamia nut borer, and scale insects. Diseases are husk spot, phytophthora and armillaria root rot.

Harvesting and use of nuts

Freshly harvested nuts have high moisture content in both the husk and the rest of the nut, which needs to be removed quickly to prevent mould. Nuts are first dehusked and dried to remove some of the moisture before the next stages of processing. Drying machines are used to remove most of the remaining moisture (down to about 1.5%) from the nuts before they are shelled. Many Australian macadamia nuts are sent to China where labour is cheaper for cracking and shelling by hand. A new nut-cracking machine has been developed in Australia and is being trialled this year; it cuts a ring around the nut shell and the nut and kernel are separated by suction devices that pull the cut shell apart. This will allow production of good quality kernels with no cracking or bruising and with no shell residue.

Macadamia nuts have the capacity to reabsorb moisture so once shelled and the kernels graded, they need to be carefully packaged to prevent their turning rancid or going mouldy. This packaging usually involves vacuum sealing in plastic or aluminium. Kernels can also be frozen.

Macadamia nuts are marketed salted or unsalted, roasted or unroasted, and are used in an increasing variety of products including macadamia icecream.

The macadamia has a high oil content, as much as 72%. Macadamia nut oil is excellent in salad dressings and for other culinary uses. The nuts provide some protein (although not as much as some of the other tree nuts) but contain very little starch. They provide essential amino acids, minerals, vitamins A, B1, B2, B3, carbohydrates, calcium, phosphorous and iron. Macadamia nuts are said to be good for reducing cholesterol levels with some research results estimating that 40 g of macadamia nuts taken daily will have a significant effect.

The husks from macadamia nuts are used as mulch material and to prepare compost.

Cultivars

Many trees are grown from seed. Some newly selected grafted commercial cultivars that have been given numbered names (which refer to original row plantings) are also becoming available and include A263, 'Daddow', A4, A16, A38 and 849.

Pecans (hickory)

Carya illinoinensis

The pecan (family *Juglandaceae*) was once classified as belonging to the *Juglans* genus, the same as walnuts, and although the nut has lots of similarities with the walnut, the species has now been reclassified. The pecan is a deciduous tree native to North America with its name coming from the indigenous Americans, the Algonquins, and meaning 'nut requiring stone to crack'. The related eastern and central North American species, the shagbark hickory (*C. ovata*), the shellback hickory (*C. laciniosa*), the mockernut (*C. tomentosa*), and also the pignuts (*C. glabra*, *C. ovalis*) are others in this group, mostly with sweet nuts that have as yet to be commercialised. Many of these related species have the potential to produce good timber as well as edible nuts.

The pecan needs specific growing and climatic conditions to crop well but will grow successfully as an ornamental garden tree outside the preferred 'ideal' areas. In Australia, pecan nut trees grow in selected areas near Perth (WA), Moree, Lismore, Hunter Valley, Grafton (NSW), Gympie, Childers, Yelarbon (Queensland) and Robinvale (Victoria). I have seen trees growing and fruiting as far south as Bendigo in inland Victoria but the trees grew very small and in some seasons the nuts failed to mature. Grafton, in New South Wales, has pecan nut trees grown as street trees; they make magnificent specimen trees and supply free nuts to town residents.

WALDORF SALAD WITH PECANS

1 cup unpeeled apples, diced or
   finely sliced
1 cup sliced celery
1 cup pecan nuts
1/2 cup grapes or yostaberries
1/2 cup mayonnaise (could use nut
   mayonnaise)

Mix all together and garnish with fresh green mint or parsley. Can be served individually on a bed of green lettuce leaves garnished with extra pecan nuts and green mint leaves or parsley.

Australia has the largest commercial pecan production outside the US, with most occurring in NSW.

Care and maintenance

The pecan tree prefers deep well-drained soils and for fruit set requires several hundred hours of temperatures under 7.5°C (45°F). It is similar to many peach cultivars in this respect. For the pecan nuts to grow well to maturity the trees need long, dry, frost-free days; depending upon cultivar this varies from 140 to over 200 days. Pecans also have quite specific temperature requirements: the ideal yearly average temperature is 24-30°C (75-86°F). Although trees can withstand areas of humidity above 80% in semi-tropical regions this can reduce cropping potential.

Pecans produce male catkin-like structures and swollen-stemmed female flowers with tiny, fluffy pollen receptors; the pollen is blown by the wind to effect pollination. Pecans can self-pollinate, that is one tree growing by itself can produce nuts (see Glossary). With some cultivars the catkins that produce the pollen may release it at a time when the female flower part is not receptive, or after it was ready for pollination, resulting in failure to form nuts. To overcome this problem commercial growers plant two or more cultivars. At 'Trawalla', a 730-ha orchard near Moree in NSW, they have planted two main cultivars, 'Witchita' and 'Western Schley'. 'Witchita' tends to shed its pollen before female flowers are receptive while 'Western Schley' sheds afterwards. By combining the two cultivars the pollen-shedding overlaps and ensures that the flowers of both cultivars receive pollen and will crop successfully.

Pecan nut (*Carya illinoinensis*) flower catkins

Pecan nuts (*Carya illinoinensis*) forming, Carisbrook, Victoria

Propagation

Selected pecan cultivars are usually budded or grafted onto seedling pecan rootstocks, using a number of methods. Grafting with dormant scions can be done in spring when the stock plant has begun growth. If this is attempted too early, branches may bleed sap profusely, so it is recommended that scions be stored until the tree has reached the correct stage.

Once the bark of the rootstock begins to slip easily when lifted, it is the best time for successful grafting. The types of graft used on pecan trees include bark grafts, inlay grafts and whip grafts. Of the different methods of summer budding, patch budding and various forms of chip budding are used. Summer budding can be done with dormant stored scion material, or current season's growth can be used as a source for buds.

Pecan nuts (*Carya illinoinensis*) being harvested by machine, Trawalla pecan plantation, NSW

Pecan nut (*Carya illinoinensis*) ready for harvest, Trawalla pecan plantation, NSW, May 1994

Pests and diseases

Pecan nut trees grown in Australia do not have any major pests or diseases to contend with, although some insects such as the green vegetable bug may invade the tree and suck on immature nuts as they grow. At 'Trawalla' longicorn beetles have entered through pruning wounds. This problem has been partially overcome by injecting a natural pesticide into tree trunks and by training pruners to make even, non-ragged cuts to encourage limbs to heal well after pruning.

The pecan stem girdler, an Australian native insect, also gives some trouble but this pest has largely been controlled by setting up a breeding program to release millions of parasitic *Trichogramma* wasps into the orchard area. Organic sprays at selected intervals, weed control to remove insect feeding and breeding sites, and the use of biological controls such as the parasitic wasps and lacewings, as well as building up predator friendly environments, will control most insect outbreaks.

Harvesting and use

Pecan nuts are harvested in autumn and, in the home garden and small orchards, if trees are surrounded by bare ground or mown grass or lawn the nuts can be harvested as they drop. Commercial plantings, however, rely upon mechanical shaking of trees to loosen nuts and a sweeping machine that sucks them up, separates hulls and trash and collects the nuts ready for drying before processing and packaging.

As with many other nuts, pecans require a speedy initial drying process to prevent mould and discolouration. Like brazil nuts, pecans are susceptible to aflatoxin contamination (see Glossary) if not carefully handled. Because of their high oil content, they can also become rancid if not stored carefully and can be subject to insect damage. Pecans cannot be stored where ammonia is used as a refrigerant as this blackens the nut.

Pecans have a high fat content, and are high in calories. They provide carbohydrates, proteins, calcium, phosphorous, potassium,copper, manganese,vitamin C, vitamin E, the complete vitamin B range of B1, B2, B3, B5, B6, and small amounts of folic acid. Pecans can be used in similar ways to walnuts although their flavour is quite different. The nuts are highly valued in pies and confectionery products as well as in ice-cream, and in savoury dishes.

The shells of pecans have been used as a very effective mulch around trees and shrubs. As the industry expands more and more of this product may become available for home garden use, for example for garden pathways. Pecan shells have been used as poultry litter, as a filler in animal feed, and in insecticides and fertilisers. They are also used as an ingredient in carpet cleaners, as an abrasive in soaps, non-skid paints and metal polishes, as a filler in plastic wood and in some adhesives. The wood is valued as a hardwood for furniture and flooring.

The trees with their ferny foliage make excellent shade and ornamental trees.

Cultivars available in Australia include 'Apache', Cape Fear', 'Cherokee', 'Cheyenne', 'Desirable', 'Kiowa', 'Mahan', 'Mohawk', 'Pawnee', 'Shoshoni', 'Sioux', 'Tejas', 'Western Schley' and 'Witchita'.

Pecan nuts (*Carya illinoinensis*), close up, shelled and unshelled to show kernel

Pistachios

Pistacia vera

The Pistachio is a deciduous tree native to western Asia and has been grown for nut production in places such as Iran, Turkey and Syria for hundreds and hundreds of years. Pistachios belong to the plant family *Anacardiaceae*, the same as that of cashews and mangoes. They were introduced into California in the US in the 1930s and that state is now the second biggest producer of pistachios worldwide.

Pistachio nuts are not commonly grown for their fruit in home gardens in Australia because two trees are needed to produce nuts, as the male and female flowers occur on separate trees. However, they are widely grown for their beautiful autumn foliage. A related species, *P. chinensis*, is the one usually chosen for ornamental use because it has more leaflets per leaf and is more colourful in autumn.

Pistachio trees require specific climatic conditions to enable the plants to fruit well. They will grow well only in certain zones within Australian 'wheat belt' areas in all states except Tasmania and Queensland. One of the largest pistachio plantations is at Robinvale in Victoria. The most common cultivar grown (representing about 80% of all Australian commercial planting) is 'Sirora'.

Care and maintenance

The pistachio is a slow growing tree that can reach 25 m or more at maturity: trees are placed in orchard rows about 5 m apart. Weed control is essential, especially in the first few years, and this can be achieved chemically or organically, although organic approaches are recommended.

During their dormant season pistachio trees need 600-1000 hours with temperatures below 7°C to make sure they will flower successfully during the following season. When they are grown above latitude 28° they do not crop well and are not recommended for tropical zones where

there is no winter chilling. However, they can succeed outside productive areas as garden trees planted for their ferny foliage and autumn colours.

It is possible that new cultivars will be introduced into Australia that do not require such low chill temperatures and which produce nuts that do not split their shells. These would not only extend the growing areas but would lead to other products such as unshelled pistachios.

In spite of specific climatic requirements and other needs for good yields, pistachio trees are very tolerant of salt. In Western Australia, field trials have found that they can survive slightly saline irrigation water for extended periods but it is recommended that the plants' root systems are flushed regularly with fresh clean water or that a mix of clean and salty water be used. Although they tolerate salt it is not advisable to plant trees in very salty soils or to irrigate with highly alkaline water. The trees have a healthy, vigorous root system and will flourish in deep well-drained soils. They require minimal nutrient applications. They can easily be grown organically and once established need little fertiliser, but some will improve cropping.

Pistachio trees are long-lived and can survive for several hundred years. To prevent their growing to their natural height they should be pruned when young to produce a many-branched tree canopy that begins

Pistachio nut tree (*Pistacia vera*) with fruits

about 1 m from the ground. This will result in a much more balanced, compact shape at maturity. Pistachio trees should not need replacing as they are not affected by many pests or diseases in Australia. Established trees can exist quite well without irrigation, just relying on rainfall, but irrigation will be needed to maintain maximum nut production. Trees will begin to produce at 4–7 years of age. Many tend to bear in alternate years, that is one heavy crop is followed by an 'off' year with fewer nuts.

Propagation

To grow your own seed, use a well-drained potting mix and deep pots to cope with the vigorous root system. Pistachio seeds need a temperature of 27°C before they will germinate. Once the seedling plants are of pencil thickness they can be grafted or budded. Grafting is usually carried out in the late winter–early spring period. Rootstock plants in pots can be placed into a greenhouse in mid-winter to promote early growth and when the growth starts, dormant scions can be placed on the trees using

Pistachio nuts (*Pistacia vera*) and foliage of tree, 'Siora' cultivar, Mildura

a whip graft. Budding of plants grown outside in nursery rows is usually done in January and the 'T' bud method the most successful, with buds for budding being selected from the terminal shoots of known cultivars (see pp. 71–85 on grafting).

When the pistachio is grown from seed both male and female trees are produced, but the difference can be distinguished only at the time of blossoming. Male flowers have red anthers and are covered in pollen; the female flowers have stigmas which turn a reddish colour at the stage that they become receptive to pollen. Female flowers occur in large clusters of up to 200 and this is why the nuts appear in large clustered groups upon the tree.

Generally, one male pollinator tree is needed for about 10 female trees. It is important to select male trees that shed pollen at or near the time the female flowers are receptive. This is why growers usually select two pollinators, one that flowers just before and one that flowers just after the main blooming period of the selected female cultivars. The tiny female flowers are wind-pollinated and battery operated 'blowers' have been used to help distribute pollen through the trees at blossoming. Another option is to graft a single male piece (scion) onto each tree to ensure pollen supply.

Commercial growers graft selected cultivars onto seedling trees to obtain more trees for their orchards. Home gardeners could graft a pollinator branch onto a female tree to save the need for two trees. Because the male branch grows stronger than that of the female parent tree the grafted branch may have to be kept in check by pruning or by cincturing (see Glossary) the graft branch to slow its growth rate.

Pistachio nut trees are available only as grafted trees as they are very difficult to grow from cuttings. Most nursery growers produce rootstocks by growing their own seed from harvested nuts and then grafting onto these, but recently seed of a cultivar of the American *P. integerrima* has been propagated and used as rootstock plants.

Pests and disease

Pistachio plants are not bothered by many pests or diseases but one disease that causes some concern is pistachio canker and research is currently under way to identify this organism and set out measures to control its spread.

Pistachio nuts
(*Pistacia vera*)
with husk stuck
to nuts

Harvesting and use of nuts

The pistachio of trade is the kernel of the nut that consists of two greenish cotyledon halves (see Glossary) in a thin casing (shell), the shell enclosed by an oval-shaped fleshy, astringent husk. The husk becomes pinkish coloured and looks very attractive and this is the point at which the pistachio is ready for picking. When the fruit is near maturity the husk partially separates from the casing (shell), and the shell on the best cultivars also splits open to expose the nut.

While some harvesting is done by hand, most commercial enterprises use tree-shaking equipment to make the nuts fall onto bare ground or sheets so that they can be harvested with a machine like

Pistachios make wonderful additions to stuffings for pork, chicken or turkey, particularly to stuffings made with rice. Pistachios can also be added to rice dishes such as Pilao or Biryani, or to meat or chicken loaves.

a giant vacuum cleaner, which separates husks and debris. At harvest, the nuts are kept cool, then dehusked immediately so that the tannic acid in the pink hull does not stain them. They are then dried for several weeks before processing. Like brazil nuts, walnuts and pecans, pistachios are very susceptible to aflatoxin contamination so this drying process is very important to prevent fungal growth as well as to prevent tannic staining.

The nuts are commonly roasted or salted to give an extremely tasty end product. At home, they can be boiled in salty water for a few minutes before drying. They are also used in confectionery, for making pies, cakes, icecream and desserts.

The nuts are high in carbohydrates, especially sucrose, and also in protein. The high oil content makes the pistachio highly nutritious. Pistachio nuts also provide calcium, phosphorous, potassium, iron, magnesium and traces of copper. They have a high vitamin A content, and some vitamin B1 and B3, plus folic acid. Compared to other nuts pistachios contain the best source of iron, vitamin B1 and the amino acid lysine.

The pistachio provides many other useful products including wood that is used in its home, Iran, for artifacts and implements of all kinds. The tapped stems of pistachio gives a resin that is used in paints and lacquers. The galls and parts of the fruit are used for silk dyes and the husks as a mordant and in tanneries.

Walnuts

Juglans spp.

Walnuts belong to family *Juglandaceae*, which contains about 20 species of deciduous trees from North and South America, Europe and Asian regions. The trees have compound leaves with few or many leaflets per leaf. Walnuts have both male and female flowers on the one tree. Male flowers are produced in hanging catkins and female flowers are small and globular with extended feathery growths that trap the male pollen. They may grow in pairs or, as with some species, have bunches of up to 10 flowers. Walnuts prefer deep, well-

English walnut (*Juglans regia*), home garden tree growing in poor soil, Tongala, Victoria

drained moist soils, and cool winters with long dry summer periods. The *Juglans* species discussed in this text are the ones known to have been used for nut or timber production and include the English walnut or Persian walnut (*Juglans regia*), the black walnut (*Juglans nigra*), the white walnut or the butternut (*Juglans cinerea*), and the Japanese walnut or heartnut cultivar (*Juglans ailantifolia* var. *coriformis*), grown for its unique heart-shaped nuts.

Walnuts have been collected for food for hundreds of thousands of years and this has gradually led to the growing of cultivated nut tree crops. Walnuts were called 'karuon basilikon' by the ancient Greeks which meant 'kingly nut' and expresses the significance of walnuts of all kinds in human history.

The white walnut or butternut (*J. cinerea*) grows to 30 m or more and is of North American origin. This tree has coarse, soft wood used for some furniture. It has edible nuts and a yellow–orange dye produced from the nuts' husks. It is popular in America as a home garden tree but not grown much commercially, mainly because of the preference for the English walnut (*Juglans regia*), which has bigger, thinner-shelled nuts that are easier to crack open and process. Many of the butternut cultivars produce small thick-shelled nuts that shatter when cracked, making it hard to extract the walnut 'meat' (kernel).

The Japanese walnut or heartnut (*Juglans ailianthus* var. *coriformis*) is grown for its unusual flattened heart-shaped nuts. This walnut is from Japan and China and grows to about 20 m. The normal form of *J. ailianthus* syn *J. sieboldiana* (Japanese walnut) has ovate to round nuts but is not as popular as the heartnut. The tree has many-leafletted leaves that look like the ailianthus tree (Tree of Heaven *Ailianthus altissima*). The soft wood from this tree is used for furniture and a dye is made from the bark, but it is the sweet heart-shaped nuts that are especially prized in Japan.

The English walnut (*Juglans regia*) is today the most common walnut grown commercially and specifically for nut production. Although the black walnut (*J. nigra*) is usually grown for timber or to be used as rootstock material, its nuts are harvested from timber plantation trees or from naturally occurring black walnut forest areas. Black walnut trees have large nuts and a shell that is lined and ridged, and usually very thickened and hard, making it difficult to crack open. It has a small kernel when compared to the English walnut (*J. regia*).

The English walnut (or Persian walnut) can grow into a giant spreading form 30 m or more tall, and just as wide if given the growing space. There are natural forests of this tree in a large area extending from eastern Europe to the foothills of the Himalayan Mountains from where it is thought to have originated. The exact origin of this tree has been

lost in antiquity; it is one of the food-producing trees that can be traced back throughout known history and was transported from place to place along ancient trade routes, establishing itself wherever the climate and soil were suitable. There are many variations of seedling forms of this tree and because it has been so widely spread throughout the world some strains of the walnut have been developed that show distinct differences such as early or late leafing habit, large or small nuts, low growing or tall trees, and terminal flowering habits compared to lateral flowering. This tree is prized for its magnificent wood, its nuts and for home garden planting where space is available.

The English walnut was introduced into Australia by early settlers and grown in areas that were thought climatically suitable. There is a large walnut tree that was probably grown from seed still standing in the garden area of Port Arthur in Tasmania and another at 'Waterview' property on Bruny Island, also in Tasmania, that is reputed to have been planted around 1830.

The variation in Australian climatic conditions meant that English walnuts were not initially grown very widely in Australia. Most early trees were grown from seed but new cultivars (grafted plants) were gradually imported and trialled in various parts of the continent. The imported walnut trees were grafted onto seedlings of the English walnut or the black walnut.

Care and maintenance

English walnut trees are deciduous, have a ferny leaf and bear catkins (male flowers) and pistilate (female) flowers on the same tree.

Walnut trees have different male and female parts but because they are produced on the same tree do not need different cultivars for cross-pollination. The male pollen producer is a hanging catkin that releases pollen throughout the tree to be received by the tiny, antler-like, feathery structure at the end of a small, swollen, egg-shaped lump which is the receptive female part that, once pollinated, will grow into a walnut.

Often the pollen produced by the male flowers is not available to the receptive female flower; this means that only a few fruit (nuts) form, so growing at least two different cultivars is the common commercial practice to get the best crops possible. However, one single tree is quite capable of producing a large crop of walnuts providing the tree has about 800 hours of chilling in winter at temperatures around 10°C, and so long as the disease walnut blight does not become too prevalent.

English walnut (*Juglans regia*) fruit ready for picking, with split husk

Walnut trees are relatively easy to grow, but they do have specific requirements. For example, they have very large, deep root systems, especially when grown *in situ* from seed. They require very deep, well-drained soils, a cool climate in winter and relatively warm, rain-free summers, but do require moisture for growth. Despite these preferences, I have seen a walnut tree growing in heavy clay soils under conditions that provided a fairly dry root zone (the roots were able to grow under a nearby slab of concrete where waterlogging rarely occurred). The tree grew to over 20 feet tall (7 m) and just as wide, cropped prolifically and lived for over 40 years.

Young trees obtained bare-rooted or in pots from a plant nursery should be planted in late autumn or early winter to allow the plant to build up new fibrous roots as their roots will have been severely pruned when dug from the nursery field. However, if the tree has been propagated by tissue culture methods it will then have a fibrous root system. Walnuts must be planted where the soil is well drained and does not become flooded during the winter period.

If planting into clay or heavy soils trees should be placed into a high mound to prevent damage to the root system during winter rains. A small amount of fertiliser can be applied to the newly planted trees to improve growth and the whole root area should be drenched with one of the liquid seaweed products to encourage new fibrous roots.

Early plantings of walnuts were placed 30 m or more apart, but the modern trend is to plant closer to have a dwarfing effect on trees. The use of modern cultivars that flower within the first three to four years is recommended for close planting schemes.

Some gardeners never prune, thus allowing the tree to obtain its natural rounded shape. To improve the shape and lower the maximum height of the tree, however, pruning can be done during the first and second seasons to create lots of limbs, thereby reducing the tree's potential height. Pruning must be done in early winter because late pruning will cause excessive sap bleeding that may be detrimental to tree growth.

I have seen good flower bud and spur formation on a 'Wilson's Wonder' walnut piece-grafted onto a black walnut tree. The late summer pruning encouraged the formation of short spurs with flower buds. Although no scientific trials have been done using late summer pruning it is worthwhile trying this system to build up flower bud formation at an early stage to slow tree growth and encourage early crop production. Pruning is not recommended when the trees become mature unless it is absolutely necessary, although sometimes older trees that are in decline need to be pruned hard to help regeneration.

If a healthy walnut tree is suddenly pruned on one side of it, or a few limbs are removed for some reason, this seems to invigorate it and promote strong growth and long, strong new branches will grow from the pruned site during just one year. These new shoots can be summer pruned to create a more branching habit, but are best left unpruned for several years to allow the tree to settle down.

Even though mature trees do not need as much pruning, sometimes those that have been left untended for years may need some attention as they become woody, with dead and dying limbs with sparse leaf formation. In such cases, it is important to try to get the tree growing again, to supply it with food and water and to build up the biological activity within the surrounding soil. Rejuvenation can be done at any time but is probably best begun in the winter–spring period. The following is a step-by-step method to successfully rejuvenate old walnut trees that are in need of care:

Lightly prune the tree, taking out all dead twigs and dead small branches; these can be recognised from their withered grey appearance. Be wary of removing very large limbs over 50 mm in diameter because weakened walnut trees do not seem to respond well to heavy pruning of large branches and they are liable to bleed sap readily from the wound site.

If more than half of the original foliage area has been removed it

CORIANDER PESTO

Good bunch of fresh coriander
2 good cloves of fresh garlic
200 g walnuts (shelled)
Parmesan or romano cheese to taste
Pepper to taste

Blend all ingredients in a food processor with just enough olive oil to make a smooth paste. A drop or two of walnut oil can also be added. Use to accompany Moroccan dishes such as Moroccan lamb shanks or vegetable or fish tagines.

may be worthwhile painting the bark of the exposed trunk and large limbs with a white water-based paint to reduce sunburning during the first summer after pruning.

Aerate the soil from the trunk outwards to well past the edge of the foliage area by drilling small augur holes every 40–50 mm or by forking the whole area to the depth of the garden fork. If an augur is used drill random holes at varying depths of between 200-500 mm.

Cover the aerated area with compost, shredded organic waste, hay or pea straw to a depth of about 200 mm, making sure that the mulch material is no deeper than 50-100 mm around the tree trunk to avoid collar rot.

Thoroughly soak the hay and soil with water. Wait a few hours then soak the area again with a mix of water containing one of the liquid seaweed products such as Maxicrop™. The seaweed product will help initiate new fibrous root growth. A light application at the same time of a complete fertiliser will also aid in rejuvenating tree health. The walnut tree may take two seasons to recover and become productive but it will be worth the wait.

Propagation

Although walnut trees can be grown easily from seed, and they may come fairly 'true to type' (see 'Seedling variation' in Glossary), they take a very long time to start fruiting. It is best, therefore, to buy or produce grafted plants that will yield nuts within 3–5 years after planting.

Specific walnut tree cultivars are usually grafted onto seedling walnuts of the same species or onto seedlings of the black walnut. In areas with

FAR LEFT:
Butternut or
white walnut
(*Juglans cineria*)
nuts showing
walnut blight

LEFT: Butternut
or white walnut
(*Juglans cineria*)
foliage showing
erinose mite
damage

LEFT: English
walnut (*Juglans
regia*) nuts
showing
damage by
dried fruit moth
larvae

FAR LEFT:
English walnut
(*Juglans regia*)
nuts affected by
walnut blight

warm spring weather the ordinary whip and tongue graft can be used. Scion wood can also be gathered in winter and stored in a sealed plastic bag or wrapped in moist newspaper in the crisper section of a home refrigerator until needed. The grafting can be done during the December–January period with success. One of the most common approaches is to use patch budding at the end of a growth cycle during mid-summer. Chip budding can also be used providing that the 'chip' shape fits the wound area exactly (for further detail see pp. 71–85 on grafting).

Recently walnut trees have been successfully propagated by tissue culture and these will gradually become available to home gardeners.

Walnut cultivars of *J.regia* that have been trialled in Australia and may become available to home gardeners if they prove to be successful include: 'Amigo', 'Ashley', 'Concord', 'Chandler', 'Chico', 'Cisco', 'Eureka', 'Franquette', 'G.N. 26' and 'G.N. 139', 'Gustine', 'Hartley', 'Howard', 'Kumnick Pride', 'Lara', 'Lompoc', 'Mayette' ('Treyve Mayette'), 'Payne', 'Placentia', 'Serr', 'Sunland', 'Tehama', 'Vina', 'Wilson's Wonder' and 'Wybellina'.

Pests and diseases

It is interesting to note that the walnut tree growing at Port Arthur shows signs of walnut blister mite infection and walnut blight that could have been picked up from a previously introduced walnut tree; these are two of the most common problems associated with walnut culture.

Walnut blight (*Xanthomonas campestris pv. juglandis*) is a bacterial disease which can be very damaging to walnut crops and in some years can reduce cropping substantially. It is spread by wind and rain. The disease shows as water-soaked areas on leaves and catkins and eventually black spots occur. Leaves will become distorted in shape and developing fruit may shrivel. If the disease is less severe the husk tightens around the nut and fails to fall and the nuts may have rotted kernels. Young shoots will develop black spots that can girdle and kill them.

Control by spraying copper oxychloride or Bordeaux at bud burst and then at regular intervals. It is also a good idea to remove all dead and infected twigs and shoots during the winter to prevent the build-up of spores within the tree. Large trees are difficult to manage because the sprays must cover all of the tree to enable adequate control. Some home gardeners opt for a non-chemical spray and grow organically by using only materials recommended by organic gardening and farming organisations.

Walnut blister mites (*Eriophyes tristriatus*) are tiny and feed on the underside of leaves, producing a furry-like patch and causing distorted lumpy growth (blisters) on the leaves' upper surface. Leaves may also become very distorted. The mite can be controlled with the organic spray lime sulphur if it is applied just before bud burst.

Immature walnut nuts may, at times, be attacked by codling moth and should be treated for this in the same way as apples (see my *All About Apples*, Hyland House, 2001).

Harvesting and use of nuts

In a good season with no walnut blight to reduce cropping, a large tree can produce a prodigious crop of nuts up to 50 kg or more.

Walnuts are usually harvested as they fall from the tree or at a time the husks start splitting from the shell, but in commercial operations the nuts are shaken from the tree with a mechanised shaker. Home gardeners can harvest when they see the outside shell of the nut (husk) start to split. Dehusk and then dry the nuts which will store for a year or more before developing a rancid sour off-taste. Some gardeners pick the developing nuts at an early immature stage before the inside nut hardens so as to be able to pickle the whole nut. Pickled walnuts have their own distinctive taste relished by some, and used sliced as a savoury dish.

Walnuts are high in moisture when they are picked and need to be dried carefully to avoid moulds and rancidity. They are high in fats and oils; walnut oil is extracted and used in cooking and is excellent salad for dressings. Second pressing of seed oil is also used in paint, printing ink and for the manufacture of soap. The residue can be used for stock-food. Walnut shells are used as a filler in much the same ways as the shells of pecan nuts. Extremely finely ground shells are used in insecticides and as an abrasive for cleaning jet aircraft engines.

Walnuts provide many calories, contain carbohydrates, protein, fats, calcium, phosphorous, potassium, small amounts of sodium and iron, magnesium, copper, manganese, zinc, vitamin A, some vitamin C, vitamin E, all the vitamin B group including B1, B2, B3, B5, B6, and some biotin and folic acid.

Soft immature walnut husks provide an excellent dye material, especially those from the white walnut or butternut (*Juglans cinerea*).

Propagation

methods for nut trees

There are several methods of propagating nut tree species: from seed, by budding and grafting, from cuttings, by aerial layering and layering, and by tissue culture. Growing from seed is relatively easy but there are problems with this as I will explain below. Seedlings grown from seed may, however, be used to graft onto, applying some of the budding and grafting methods outlined.

Even though not all nut trees lend themselves to propagation by cuttings, I deal with this method in detail so that home gardeners can experiment for themselves. Layering and aerial layering can be used used to propagate some tree nuts, particularly macadamias and hazelnuts (filberts), and the lychee (see next section), and these methods are also explained in detail.

New technology has allowed commercial laboratories to begin mass producing almond and walnut cultivars using tissue culture techniques, where pieces of tissue from any selected plant cultivar are grown in test tubes or flasks to produce clumps of tiny virus-free identical plants or rootstocks. This approach is one that is of increasing interest to commercial nut growers, and the trees developed by this method will become available for home gardeners to purchase.

Growing from seed

The most common way to propagate many species of tree nuts is by seed. This is not a reliable method, however, because it often gives rise to a large number of cultivars instead of plants that are all the same. Each seedling, although it may be very similar (true to type) to the parent plant, will be to some degree genetically different. These genetic differences may show up in the new cultivars' ability to produce good crops, in the size of the nuts, in the thickness of the shell, in the recoverable

shell–kernel ratio, or in the size of the plant. Shape or form may also differ or the seedlings may have early or late cropping and flowering times (see Glossary on seedling variation). Seedlings will also take a longer time to start cropping compared with budded or grafted plants. Another problem with seedling variation is the individual plant's susceptibility or resistance to pests and diseases.

For the home gardener growing a nut tree from seed can be a challenge and very rewarding, but for commercial purposes all plants must develop into regular trees that will yield crops of nuts of uniform quantity and quality. Seedling variation can also lead to confusion over cultivars and cultivar names (see Hazelnuts).

Most tree nuts can be grown from seed in a seedling potting medium, using techniques adapted from the trees' natural setting. In a natural forest environment, the seeds (nuts) fall from the trees and are covered in a mulch of leaves or forest debris. Rain wets the forest floor and gradually the fallen nuts are effected by moisture and spring–summer warmth which initiates seed germination and plant growth. This may take just a few months or several years. Animals such as squirrels collect and bury nuts and some of those they forget germinate and grow into trees or shrubs. Because of the hard shell some nuts will pass right through an animal or bird's digestive system; this weakens or breaks the shell so that germination can take place more readily. Other nuts just pass through the animal and are deposited with a large dollop of dung which provides food for the germinating seedling.

These natural processes sometimes need to be emulated in preparing nuts for germination. Those such as the macadamia from warm climate areas can be gathered at harvest, dehusked and then planted directly into pots or into soil and the hard seed coat (shell) will split and allow the kernel (seed) to germinate. Nuts such as chestnuts, which originate in cold areas, need cold treatment (a vernalisation period) before they are planted out. Placing seeds in a cool part of a refrigerator at a temperature just above freezing will achieve this and allow the seeds to germinate easily. For nuts that need this treatment the refrigerated period is usually 2–3 months.

Almond seeds can be prepared by the above method, but an alternative to storing the whole nuts, thus saving space, is to crack them open, extract the uninjured kernels, dust them with a copper fungicide such as Bordeaux and then lay them in damp sand inside a container, which is then placed in the refrigerator. Extracting the kernels first often gives better results because fewer seeds are lost to rotting organisms. After the cool period the almond kernels are planted into a sterile medium such as perlite, vermiculite, special seedling mixes or copra peat (recycled coconut fibre) and grown on for one year before planting out into the field or using for rootstock material. Although seed can be planted directly into soil most growers plant into pots. Germinating seedlings inside a greenhouse or shadehouse or on a protected bench with basal heating will speed the process and give best results.

Seedling plants grown for use in the garden can be transplanted directly from their pots to their final position after one year's growth or when the plant reaches 20–30cm in height. Staking and the use of a tree guard is recommended until the plant becomes established.

Seedlings grown for rootstock material should be gradually 'potted up' until they are in pots of about 25 cm in diameter. The plants should be fed with a granular, or preferably an organic, fertiliser or given frequent liquid feeds. This will help them grow to the size required for success. Most nut species are budded or grafted to fairly large rootstock material with a stem diameter of 100 mm or more.

Budding and grafting

The most common and reliable way to reproduce identical plants is by budding and grafting.

The successful cultivation of most fruit tree cultivars and varieties — including nuts — relies upon the fact that they can be propagated by these methods: the transfer of a bud or buds, or a piece of growth con-

1. English Walnut
(Juglans regia),
seedling and nut
2. Pistachio nuts
(Pistacia vera)
germinating in
propagation pots

taining several buds (scion), from one tree to another (rootstock), thus producing identical trees growing the same fruit, and allowing the establishment of a uniform orchard.

Home gardeners can be reasonably certain of success when grafting or budding at almost any time of the year. All they have to do is use a little new technology and follow a few simple guidelines and techniques and the process is as simple as reciting ABC.

Equipment: The major component of the grafting–budding operation is the equipment. Knives and secateurs must be very, very sharp and clean. This will allow a clean cut edge and quick callusing (see Glossary) at the graft point and prevent disease contamination of the graft area. One way to check your knives or secateurs for sharpness is to lightly run the cutting edge of a knife blade along a sheet of newspaper, or use the usual cutting action with the secateurs. If a clean cut results the blade edge is sharp enough for use; if you have a rough cut or torn paper, then re-sharpen the cutting edge. Knives and secateurs should be cleaned and sharpened regularly.

To cut the buds a very sharp budding knife is recommended, but one-sided razor blades, extremely sharp kitchen knives, fruit knives and pocket knives have been used by home gardeners who do not have access to expensive budding knives. It is important, though, to sharpen only one side of the blade on any of these cutting tools; a V-shaped cutting edge tends to rip the bark and make ragged edges on any cut material. This may cause poor grafts to form.

Once the graft is done whatever method is used, completely seal it at the graft point by wrapping with budding tape or cling wrap, or by sealing with grafting wax. Tape or cling wrap can be removed when the graft has taken. To ensure a very high success rate, gardeners should place a narrow plastic sleeve over the graft scion, or chip bud and graft union area. I have developed the use of this sleeve to help ensure grafting success. The top of the sleeve is sealed and the bottom is open-ended; the base is left open to allow air to circulate within the tube. Before placing this sleeve over a graft union area, spray a few droplets of water into it with an ordinary spray bottle. The plastic sleeve acts as a humidifier and mini-greenhouse, prevents the graft from drying out and protects it from any extreme weather conditions, thus providing an environment conducive to grafting success.

Anchor the loose, hanging plastic sleeve with a pin or piece of grafting wax to prevent it blowing around. It can be left on until the graft piece starts growing, or removed when its new shoots reach the top of the inside of the sleeve. In very hot weather the enclosed leaves on the graft piece may burn (especially when scions with leaves still attached are

Removing a bud for budding an English walnut (*Juglans regia*)

Sticky tape and plastic sleeve used to make propagating sleeves for grafting.

Multi-grafted hazelnut tree (*Corylus avellana*), using plastic sleeve method

used). Damage can be avoided if the grafts are shaded or the plastic sleeve is covered with a paper bag for a short time. If the tape at the top of the plastic sleeve comes unstuck and the graft shoot grows through the top of the sleeve, ensure that the hot sun does not burn the foliage.

Besides maintaining the moisture regime, plastic sleeves provide protection from insects, animals and weather and keep the graft warmer, which in turn encourages quicker callus formation at the graft union. I have successfully grafted new shoots onto new growth and used various forms of grafting by utilising the plastic sleeve system from winter right through to April. Even old bud sticks that have started to shoot and grow have been used with success. Plastic sleeves can be used to cover any type of graft and the graft will benefit. Their use means that traditional methods of grafting can be adapted and expanded upon. For instance, gardeners can now have just one bud instead of the traditional 4–6 buds per cutting (scion) or select up to 1m length scions for grafting purposes and still have success.

The ideal type of plastic sleeve can be made from tubular packaging material manufactured for packing small items: this can be bought in huge rolls for very little cost. It is even more economical to cut and stitch up recycled clear, white or opaque plastic to make into narrow plastic bags for the purpose. The plastic sleeves can be made from bubble plastic for extra warmth and this may be important for some nut species such as hazelnuts. Materials such as stretch parafilm (a medical self-sticking wrapping plastic that can be moulded around the graft) will also work well.

Ties are also an important part of budding and grafting equipment. Not so long ago the only material available for securing and tying grafts was raffia or string but now there are many more to choose from. New products such as perishable rubberised strips, plastic budding tape, waxed string, sealing waxes and petroleum-based waxes, as well as clamps, pegs, sealing tape and stretch plastic such as glad wrap and parafilm all help to ensure success with budding and grafting operations. For those with little money to spend on special budding tape an alternative is recycled bicycle or car tyre tubes cut into strips to tape all grafts. The rubber strip expands with the growing graft union and will eventually perish, so there is no real need to remove the tie.

Budding: Budding is actually a form of grafting, and can be described as lifting the 'skin' (bark) of a small branch or lateral and placing a live bud under it so that it forms a graft. When the limb is cut back to the inserted bud, thus causing the bud to grow, this growth shoot will eventually produce the same sort of fruit as that of the tree from which the bud was taken. Historically, traditional spring or summer budding has been seen as a separate function from the traditional winter–spring grafting, probably because budding was done at a different time of the year and involved using tiny pieces of graft material compared to winter–spring scion grafting where large pieces of shoots may be used.

Traditional budding is usually done at the end of the growth period of the plant to be budded. In simple terms, this means that you usually do budding in late summer or after a growth flush when there are no more new leaves appearing on the plant shoots. Chip budding is an exception to this rule as it can be done at almost any time regardless of whether the bark lifts easily or not.

Scions: 'Scion' is the name given to a piece of the bud stick chosen for grafting. Usually there are 5–10 buds on a scion 10–20 cm long. These scion pieces have leaves attached when taken from evergreen nut species or are devoid of leaves when taken in winter from deciduous nut trees, such as almonds and chestnuts. Some grafters cut in half any leaves attached to the scion to be grafted, or remove most of them. This is not essential if a plastic sleeve is used to cover the graft. Gardeners can prepare the scion with only one bud or 100 buds and still get good results, provided a plastic humidifying sleeve is used to cover the graft (dealt with in detail later in this chapter). The use of one-bud scions is ideal when bud wood is scarce or the plant to be propagated is very rare.

The choice of plant material to be used for budding and grafting can influence the success or failure of the operation. Material should be cut from the donor plant from areas where it is exposed to full sunlight and from where it fruits well. Sometimes with plants that are difficult to graft (especially thin-growthed evergreens) try ring-barking below the shoot you are going to harvest for bud sticks for a short period before collection. This builds up the plant sugar reserves in the shoot and often results in grafting success when these scions are used. Another method of ensuring that stock plant material has a greater success rate when you use it for stem propagation or for budding and grafting is to reduce the amount of light to the plant (see etiolation in Glossary) for about 3–4 weeks by using heavy (50% or more) shadecloth covering. The plant is then allowed full sunlight for a week before you take cuttings or graft material from it.

Dormant material such as that used for almonds, walnuts and chestnuts can be gathered in the autumn–winter period and stored for later use, depending on when the budding or grafting is to take place (usually during springtime). Collect pieces that are about 20 cm long and prepare them by cutting the bottom of the shoots diagonally to identify the base and avoid placing grafts upside down onto rootstocks, when they certainly will not grow.

The cut budsticks (scion material) can be bundled and secured with a tie or rubber band and then placed inside a sealed plastic bag which has had most of the air squeezed out of it. For extra long storage you can place another black plastic bag or wrapping around the original bundle to exclude any light. It is a good idea to spray a mist of water inside of the bag and onto the cuttings before sealing it. The packaged bag can then be stored in the crisper section of the refrigerator until needed.

Scion material can be stored for six months or more if dormant material is needed for summer grafting, as sometimes is the case for walnuts or almonds. Collected evergreen material such as that used for macadamia budding and grafting is usually cut from the donor plant at the time of the operation but it is also possible to store this material for a week or more inside a sealed and 'misted' plastic bag placed in the crisper section of the refrigerator (or in an 'esky' or some other cool dark place).

When you take the budsticks to use for budding and grafting they can be cut into 2–5 bud pieces (scions) if necessary. Different grafting methods are used for various nut plant species, and often the chosen grafting method depends on the time of year of the operation and the type of graft material (budwood) available at the time. Grafting is traditionally done during the spring or summer period, and budding in spring, summer or late summer.

'T' budding: There are various ways of making a cut into a limb (rootstock) to enable the grafter to lift the bark. The system most used is a 'T' cut into a limb or shoot that has grown during the previous summer season or, as with some nut species, a 2–3-year-old tree trunk. It is made by using two cuts at right angles to each other, in the shape of a capital letter 'T'. You can then force a pointed instrument (the bump on a budding knife) or the knife edge in at the 'T' junction, pressing downwards and sideways along the cut so that the bark lifts easily if it is the right time to bud. (If the bark will not lift readily then budding cannot be done at this stage.) Lift the bark along both sides of the vertical part of the 'T'. It is then ready for the bud to be inserted.

Insert the base of the shield bud (see below for details on cutting buds) under the bark along the horizontal bar of the 'T'. Move the bud downwards until the flaps of bark formed either side of the vertical cut partially close back over it. Make sure that the inserted bud clears the bar of the 'T' or cut the bud shield so that it does not overlap the bar. Then tie the bud in place with string, plastic budding tape, rubberised tape, raffia or other material. It is important that the tie covers and holds in the horizontal part of the 'T' cut and that the wrapping covers most of the cut area. The bud itself must be left uncovered for best results as this allows the bud to 'breathe'. Some operators actually cover the bud completely with tape, but if you do this the tape must be removed early.

Demonstration of 'T' budding

1. English walnut (*Juglans regia*): cutting 'T' for 'T' budding and

2. 'T' bud inserted

The tape is usually removed within 3–5 weeks of budding to avoid bud dehydration or burning (cooking) by the hot sun. One tying method I have developed is to twist the tape into a string at the end of the tying operation, so that you can more easily find the end of the tape when the time comes to cut and unwrap it.

For 'T' budding, the bud sticks are usually cut 10–50 cm long (depending upon the type of material available from the tree). Remove the leaves but leave a short leaf stalk to act as a handle when you insert the bud. The traditional method of cutting the bud safely is to hold the bud stick so that buds point away from you. Place the knife edge 5–10 mm above the bud on the bud stick and, using a scalloping cutting action, cut 2–3 mm into the bark, downwards (towards you), under the bud and up the other side, 3–5 mm below the bud. This will actually cut the bud from the bud stick and produce a shield-shaped patch of bark containing the bud.

Some gardeners remove the piece of woody tissue from directly behind the bud before inserting it into the rootstock to allow more area for cambial contact. (The cambial layer is that area just under the bark and usually shows as a greenish–yellow layer between the bark and the inner wood.) This is time consuming and unnecessary as field tests have shown little difference in the percentage of successful bud grafts with or without the woody tissue. Note that chip buds with a larger woody section seem to graft well at nearly any time of year.

The bud is usually placed into the 'T' cut as soon as it is taken from the bud stick. Some gardeners cut several buds at one time and hold them in their mouth to prevent them drying out; others cut the buds from the sticks the night before and store them moistened in a jar overnight in the crisper section of the refrigerator.

There are other different forms of budding and these include the following.

Chip budding: This has become the most used method of budding. Its popularity is partially due to its adaptability, ease of operation and the fact that it seems to have no seasonal limitations so that it can be carried out at nearly any time of the year, especially in Australia.

Traditionally, a chip bud is taken from the bud stick in much the same way as cutting a shield bud for 'T' budding. The main difference is that more woody tissue is removed with the bud. The knife is placed 3–10 mm above the bud and a cut made at 30° downwards towards the operator. This cut is made 5–15 mm long, depending upon the size of the bud stick, and then the knife is pulled out. The knife is then placed about 5 mm below the bud and a cut at 45° is made downwards to intersect the first cut. This creates a chip that falls from the bud stick. If a bud touches the soil it may become infected with soil bacteria or fungi which will lead to budding failure. (This can be avoided if the action of cutting mentioned above is reversed so that the chip bud that is cut will remain on the budding knife blade and not drop to the ground or into grass.)

The exact same cut is made on the rootstock and a chip socket with the same angles is created. The chip removed is discarded. The chip bud is inserted and if the stems of the bud stick and the rootstock each have the same diameter, then the transfer of buds will give an exact fit and it will be hard to even see that the chip bud is in place. This has the advantage of more cambial layer contact so that quicker healing and grafting will take place. (If the rootstock chip bud site is large two buds can be inserted, one each side of the cut.)

The chip bud fits neatly into its socket and can be tied in place with budding tape. Usually the whole bud is covered with the tape which can be removed 3–5 weeks later when the graft should have taken. Some gardeners only partially wrap the chip bud, leaving the bud's surface open to the air. This can be done especially with chip buds taken while the plant has leaves or is an evergreen species. With this method I have developed, the chip bud is removed with a leaf or partial leaf still attached and although the leaf will eventually die it seems to give some food through photosynthesis to the developing chip bud. I have tried this method with many species, including almonds in the summer period, and it should work well with some of the evergreen nuts. If a chip bud with leaf attached is used it will need to be covered with a plastic sleeve (see below) and the limb on which the bud is inserted will have to be shortened to 10–15 cm above the insertion point to allow the placment of the plastic sleeve over the graft area (see below). To ensure better callus growth, bubble plastic can be wrapped around the budding tape that holds the chip bud;

English walnut (*Juglans regia*):

1. chip cut for chip budding

2. chip bud inserted

3. summer, inserted chip bud

4. chip bud after budding, showing bud swell

Successful chip bud
and resultant growth
shoot on an almond
tree (*Prunus dulcis*)

this gives and retains extra warmth, particularly useful for some nut species that require warmth for callus formation. It is also beneficial during generally cool weather conditions or when the nights are cold.

Experts differ about the tying of the chip bud. Some advocate using only two pieces of string, rubberised material or budding tape just to hold the bud in place, one tie above and the other below the actual bud. Others cover and seal most of the chip bud area. My experience shows that loose tying is suited to warm weather conditions while tight sealing of most of the area is advisable in cool parts of the year to protect the bud and give warmth to promote callusing. Extra good results can be obtained if a small open-ended plastic sleeve (sealed at the top) containing a little moisture is inserted over the graft area until callusing has occurred.

Patch budding: This is an older form of grafting often seen described in old gardening text books and could have been one of the first grafting techniques used. The operation can be done during spring or summer or any time that bark on the plants to be budded slips easily when cut. Walnuts and macadamia nuts can be propagated using this technique. Basically patch budding is similar to 'T' budding in that a piece of bark with a bud at its centre is transferred to a rootstock, but in the case of

Macadamia nut tree (*Macadamia integrifolia*):

1. Tools for macadamia nut grafting (punch or patch budding)

2. Grafting, using punch or patch budding on macadamia nut seedling

patch budding the 'patch' is placed into an identically shaped opening that has been cut in the bark layer of the rootstock.

A sharpened tool is used to remove the patch containing a bud. The patch can be round, oval, square or oblong. A double-bladed knife is sometimes used. The tool is pressed into the bark, wriggled slightly to dislodge the bark layer and the patch is transferred to a hole that has been made in the rootstock bark with the identically shaped tool so that the patch fits exactly at its edges. When a double-bladed knife is used two cuts across the donor budwood are made to help remove the patch, but the identical patch cut on the rootstock must be done as carefully as possible so as not to have overcut or rough edges with lifted bark.

The patch is sealed around its edges with budding tape to press the two cut edges together to form a graft. The patch bud can be completely covered or only at its edges, but total coverage allows the patch to be pressed against the cambial layer to give the patch a better chance to graft properly. The budding tape is removed after a few weeks and the rootstock cut back to the inserted patch bud during the next winter–spring period. To prepare a different type of patch follow the sequence used for marcotting (also dealt with in this chapter), but in this case a

Patch budding into
English walnut
(*Juglans regia*)

piece of bark the exact size of the one containing a bud is removed from the selected cultivar and placed into the gap opened by the bark removal operation.

Micro-budding: This method is so-called because it uses very tiny, often undeveloped, buds to graft onto tiny rootstocks with chip budding or 'T' budding; it can be done during the summer period.

Whip and tongue grafting: This is probably the easiest and most reliable way of grafting together two pieces of wood of similar size, although odd-sized pieces can also be grafted very successfully using this method, providing one side of the scion is in line with one side of the rootstock. Traditionally the grafting operation is done at the time the rootstock shows some bud movement: in deciduous species, during the spring–summer period, or after harvest with evergreen species. If a plastic sleeve is used over the graft (see below), grafting can be done at almost any time of year. Leaves on the scion material to be used can be left on, trimmed or removed. If plastic sleeves are used in hot summer conditions place a paper bag over the plastic sleeve to give some shading until the scion has grafted and the plastic sleeve removed.

With deciduous species traditional thinking dictates that the graft wood and buds be dormant at the time the graft is made. The reasoning behind this is that the dormant buds are slow to move and by the time they start to grow the graft will have formed, whereas if the buds are moving (actually growing) at the time of grafting this uses energy, res-

piration causes water loss in the inserted scion and the shoot will dehydrate and die before grafting can take place. However, plastic sleeves will allow even buds that have started to grow and open up to be used. This applies to evergreen species as well. Once a graft has formed the grafted shoot receives nourishment and water from the parent plant or rootstock.

For a traditional whip and tongue graft choose a graft piece containing 3–5 buds. The base end is cut at an angle of about 30° and the same 30° cut is made on the stock plant. If the angle is too sharp the two pieces tend to split when joined together with the whip and tongue graft, but lesser angles will allow the pieces to graft well. With some nut species such as macadamia, the sloping cut is sometimes made without the 'tongue'.

For the whip and tongue a splitting downward cut is made 5–15 mm into the 30° surface of each cut. It is important that one cut is made one-third of the way along the surface of the 30° cut and the other made half-way along the other 30° cut. This is necessary so that when the two sloping edges are forced together the tongue parts will join and fit neatly to form a perfect union. If the splitting cuts are made at the same point along each of the 30° cut surfaces, then the graft area will overlap and a poor graft will form. If the graft piece and rootstock are the same diameter, and the procedure is well done, you will hardly see the graft when it is completed.

Bark grafts: There are at least two commonly used bark grafts: one is the insertion of graft scions into the end of cut limbs; the other is insertion of graft scions under the bark into an L-shaped cut made into bark on the side of a branch, which is similar to side grafting.

Mr Jim Martin grafting pistachio nut trees, using a whip graft.

Bark grafts are made into the cut end of a limb by simply making one or two knife cuts to the depth of the bark layer away from the limb's cut edge. Usually the cuts are 10–30 mm long. If a double cut is made the distance between cuts is about 10 mm. When a double cut is used, a sharp instrument, budding knife, or a clean sharp screwdriver end can be inserted at the area between the bark and inner wood and the bark will lift away as a flap. When only one cut is made a screwdriver or special grafting 'bump' (found on some budding/grafting knives) is forced between the bark and inner wood at the cut and this loosens the bark a little to enable insertion of the scion. The one cut system is best used for trees or limbs with thin bark to lessen the damage caused by the cuts.

A scion is chosen and one edge cut at about 30° or less to obtain a thinned sloping wedge. This can be cut at the base to form a chisel point for easy insertion. This end is then slid between the bark and wood, and then the area taped or sealed with grafting wax. Alternatively a small nail or tack can be hammered in to keep the scion in place, then the graft waxed. The placement of a plastic sleeve over the graft is recommended for both dormant and evergreen scions.

Green grafting: The use of new, soft, green growing shoots as scions for grafting during the spring–summer period, or 'green grafting', is not well documented. In the past, this method has not been used much because the graft pieces tended to dry out within hours of grafting and to dehydrate before the graft could take. With the use of the plastic sleeve as described above the problem of scion dehydration is solved.

Active green shoots actually graft very quickly, are more resilient because they have younger growth cells that form callus very rapidly, and once grafted will grow extremely well. However, if the grafting is done late in the season the graft may not really grow much until the following spring. For some home gardeners, the only small worry about green grafting is that the pieces used are tiny; however, the operation is easier. All you do is cut the top off a growing shoot on the tree to be grafted; cut the stub that is left down the centre to about 10–15 mm. Then cut the topmost shoot off a lateral from the scion (donor) tree, remove the lower leaves, cut the bottom end of the shoot into a V point. When very soft scion shoot material is used the scion top can be pinched out before grafting. The scion is then inserted into the cut in the shoot on the rootstock tree.

The green graft can be tied, held with a peg or grafting mastic or stuck through with a pin; a narrow, moisturised, open-ended plastic bag is placed over the graft and pinned, then left until the growth of the shoot touches the top of the plastic sleeve or the scion has grafted. Extremely soft shoots sometimes die at the tip but the base section will still remain alive.

The goat's foot graft: This is used when only small diameter rootstock is available and the scion wood has a very large diameter; it can be used for deciduous plants or evergreens. The rootstock is prepared by cutting it down the centre for about 4 cm. The scion is prepared by slicing two sides of the round shoot so that the cuts form a trianglular shape; bark is left on the base edge of the triangle. The two cuts are continually whittled away until only a thin strip of bark and a tiny triangular-shaped stem piece are left. The thin stem section is then inserted sideways into the cut rootstock until the bark layer matches and then the whole graft is tied and sealed; a plastic sleeve placed over the graft, especially with evergreen species.

Multi-grafting: Keen home gardeners may like to try multi-grafting where three or more scions of different cultivars are joined together and then this joined piece is grafted to the nut tree. The use of a plastic sleeve (see below) is essential if this graft is used.

Root grafting: During winter to early spring this can be done to multiply the number of trees grafted with some species. Root grafting is done by placing a scion of the selected variety–cultivar onto a piece of cut root section. The graft is sealed with wax, the pieces partially buried in propagation media and given warmth until the graft has taken, then the plants are potted up or planted directly into the home orchard.

Scion graft and rootstock cuttings: This can be done with nut species that have rootstocks that readily form roots from cuttings. If the scion and rootstock piece are grafted together, covered with a plastic sleeve (see below), then placed into a propagation mix, they will graft and grow into an instant grafted tree in one season. The growing medium used for propagation can be pure washed river sand, sharp river sand and 10% peat moss, or copra peat mixed with a little river sand. There are other materials to use for propagation, and choice may be determined by prices. New on the market are foam and fibre glass blocks.

Propagation from cuttings

Nearly all trees and shrubs can be propagated using stem cut[...] includes most tree nut species. Sometimes trees d[...] tings grow slowly compared to grafted plants, o[...]

1. English walnut (*Juglans regia*), 'green graft' covered with plastic sleeve

2. Graft of hazelnut or filbert tree (*Corylus avellana*), showing uneven callus knit due to improper joining of graft piece.

root systems. Generally tree nut species are not grown from stem cut-tings for commercial purposes either because they cannot be success-fully propagated by this method or because they grow so well from seed. Macadmias and hazelnuts (filberts), however, are often grown from cut-tings, as are most evergreen tree nut species, although sometimes with difficulty. Other nuts dealt with in the following section, including gingkos and lychees, can also be grown from stem cuttings.

Stem cuttings: Growing nut trees from cuttings is a option where the plants readily adapt to this method and when the species are able to establish well on their own root systems. Many nut-producing plant cul-tivars do not, or are susceptible to disease organisms, and so are grafted onto special or seedling rootstocks.

Dormant stem cuttings: Cuttings from deciduous trees are taken in the autumn–winter period and sometimes stored in a cool room until needed, or immediately planted into pots, trays or open ground. The ideal length of cuttings is about 30-40 cm. Half or two-thirds of the cutting is poked into a propagating mix or into soil. For plants that sucker it is best to remove with a sharp knife all buds that would otherwise be below the medium or soil level. A root-promoting hormone can be applied to the base of the cuttings before insertion in the medium; some gar-deners also wound the cutting base before applying the substance. Shorter cuttings can be used if the home gardener has access to a hothouse and special propagation equipment.

Leafy stem (semi-hardened) cuttings: These are taken from growth shoots of deciduous trees during their growing phase or from evergreen trees and shrubs at any time. With fruiting trees cuttings are best taken just after cropping has finished but for propagation they can be taken at any time. The type of cutting depends on the species. Many of the more easily propagated plants can be grown from just the leaf and leaf stalk, others from short-stemmed cuttings containing one leaf, some from split-stemmed cuttings and still others from lengthy ones. The use of root-promoting l   gels or powders is optional but many evergreen plants give fa   s when such a compound is used.

have a well-drained medium into which to place
eners use perlite, peat moss, vermiculite, copra
. Moisture is essential and can be supplied by
fogging unit and it is best for most cuttings
mperatures. A glasshouse can be used for
arm regions, to provide a heated or shel-
nake your own greenhouse from recy-
an old 'Hills Hoist' clothes-line. If a

greenhouse has a double wall of plastic instead of one single layer the heat is retained for much longer.

Tip (soft wood) cuttings: These are the very top shoots from an actively growing plant stem and are also leafy cuttings. Although most of the leaves are removed, or cut in half, the growing shoot at the tip is generally not removed. Because tip cuttings are very soft, and susceptible to bruising and attack by disease organisms, they must be handled carefully, grown under fairly sterile conditions and provided with moisture at all times. However, it is easy to over-water and kill the plant shoots. Soft wood cuttings grow best under mist or in a fogging environment but can be grown inside a greenhouse or home-made greenhouse structure if very high humidity levels are provided around the cuttings. If warmth is given at the base of the propagation pots or trays then even better results will be achieved.

Propagating by layering

One way to produce more plants from a given tree is to practise the art of layering. Aerial layering, the rooting of stems or branches still attached to the above-ground part of the parent tree or shrub, is used for some tree nuts that are difficult to propagate using traditional stem cuttings, or when large plants are needed relatively quickly. Marcotting is a form of aerial layering used for some species including the lychee (see next section). Ground layering (see below) involves layering low-growing pieces of growth of a tree or shrub into the ground where they form roots, thus propagating new plants.

Aerial layering: This form of propagation is similar to marcotting (see below), the main difference being that the area injured to promote root formation is smaller, usually a knife cut into the stem of the plant or a 1–3 mm cintured area (removal of bark around the stem). The treated area is then wrapped and covered the same way as in marcotting.

Marcotting: This form of aerial layering is used specifically for lychee nut tree production but can be applied to most nut species. Plants that are very difficult to root using cutting material can sometimes be propagated by marcotting. The small branch chosen to be used (usually a 1–3-year-old growth shoot) is stripped of leaves in the area to be 'doctored' (cut). Two cuts are made around the limb, or alternatively a double cut 1–5 cm wide made with two closely fitted sharp blades. The thin layer of bark between the cuts is removed completely by cut between the two ring cuts and peeling the bark a tively 'ring barking' the branch. The cuts are made

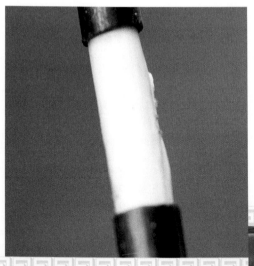

English walnut (*Juglans regia*)
showing limb prepared for
marcotting (aerial layering)

1.

2.

way, thus effec-
to the cambial layer
making a

(an indeterminate area just under the bark and often a yellowish colour). Provided the cuts are not made into the woody section of the limb this will be OK. Sometimes a root-promoting hormone is dusted or applied to the cut area. The injured area is covered with a lump (one or two small handfuls) of moist material such as moss or peat moss. This is then wrapped in clear plastic, black plastic or aluminium foil. The medium inside must not be allowed to dry out: one way of placing a few more drops of water inside the bundle without unwrapping it is to use a syringe. Roots will eventually grow from the 'marcotted' area and once these are well established the limb is cut from the parent plant just below the marcotting and the rooted branch (a new plant) is placed into a pot for growing on.

Ground layering: For this form of layering, bend a branch down to the surrounding soil and bury it, holding it down with a peg. Allow the top part of the branch to poke above ground level.

Where the branch enters the soil and turns upward make a small slit in the branch to encourage roots to grow from that point. Alternatively the branch can be cinctured by removing a very thin strip of bark from the underground section of the layered branch.

Propagation from suckers

Some trees produce suckers from the root system. Providing a nut cultivar has not been grafted onto a different rootstock and has been grown from seed or cuttings, the suckers can be cut from the root system (with some fibrous roots still attached) and used as an extra tree for the orchard. Hazelnuts (filberts) are often propagated in this way. Alternatively the sucker growth can be used as a rootstock for other cultivars to be grafted onto it.

Propagation by tissue culture

Propagation of plants by tissue culture is a relatively new science that involves producing plantlets from tissue samples, immature shoots or buds in a sterile environment so that the tiny sensitive plants are not infected with bacteria, fungi and other micro-organisms. Tissue culture has become a large horticultural business and ensures that lots of identical quality plants are produced at cheaper rates. For example, minute orchid seeds are grown on tissue culture medium to increase the number of plan~~t~~ the best possible method.

Although tissue culture laboratories have sterile roo~~m~~ powerful microscopes, immense sterilisation and he~~~ lots of capital to set up, it can be done in a li~~~

Macadamia nut tree (*Macadamia integrifolia*):
1. Seedling being prepared for marcotting
2. Marcotted tree with aerial rooting layer being tied onto trunk

such implements as pressure cookers for steam sterilisation, growth cabinets for growing plants, a greenhouse for siting plants.

There are several major steps involved with tissue culture and this is explained in very simple terms below:

- The plant material from which to propagate has to be found and made healthy to maximise propagation success.

- The cut and selected material is cleansed with sterilents such as sodium hypochlorate to get rid of any disease microbes, dirt and dust. It is then rinsed with pure water.

- Tissue material or buds or growth points are cut from the clean material and placed into a sterile medium such as an agar preparation containing salts, sugars, etc. inside a container or flask.

- Plants or tissue material are treated with, for example, growth regulators and nutrients to cause callus tissue to form (from which shoots and roots can be initiated) or to increase shoot multiplication.

- Once the number of shoots has multiplied substances that initiate root formation are applied to create a mass of roots around the plantlets.

- The plantlets are cut away into smaller clumps or as individual plants from the tissue culture clumps and separated into flasks to grow on to a manageable size before they are taken out of these containers to be potted into regular-sized pots. (Note that some tissue culture laboratories supply massed rooted plants in flasks for the recipient to care for and grow on.)

- The plants are then 'grown on' to a size ready for sale or use.

Pruning

of nut trees

runing is an essential part of nut tree care and maintenance, especially as nut trees can grow to be very large. Pruning systems can
reduce tree growth and many of these are described below. My own
system (described later in this chapter) can help contain tree growth and
produce smaller trees, and it requires less time. Trellis and espalier training systems can limit the spread of trees (mainly deciduous species) to
suit spaces in small garden areas.

Home orchards of the past were larger and designed for self-sufficiency,
but nowadays the trend is towards smaller, rarely pruned fruiting trees on
dwarfing rootstocks, while commercial planting systems are designed to
have masses of close-planted trees in very small areas. Home gardeners
have benefited from these advances.

Summer pruning is becoming very popular as an option. This applies
to lychee trees (see next section), but it can be used on other nut species,
too. Tip pruning in early summer helps double the number of branches
being formed on young trees. Pruning in late summer prevents shading
and allows more light into the developing/ripening fruit. The late summer pruning also has a secondary effect: the cut lateral stubs often produce
flower buds in the time between pruning and the following autumn, thus
ensuring fruit for the next season.

Before continuing I should make a note on cutting tools. They have
already been dealt with in the chapter on propagation but for pruning
operations it is particularly important to keep implements such as secateurs, saws, and pruning knives sharpened and clean at all times. All
cutting surfaces should be cleaned with a 10% methylated spirit–water
solution or a strong bleach, then rinsed with tap water. After pruning
diseased material, sterilise your cutting equipment before making the
next cut. Soak a rag in the cleaning solution and wipe it over the blade
to remove grunge and sap. Some diseases are easily transferred from one

branch to another and can gradually cause the death of the tree. When storing cutting equipment wipe the blades with grease or oil to inhibit rust, then store them in a dry place.

Pruning systems for nut trees

A large and varied range of systems has been developed for pruning nut trees and the choice depends on factors such as species, climate and water availability, types of rootstock used, amount of space available, soil types, and many others.

Pruning as a management approach probably evolved when growers noticed that although trees with broken branches (caused by the previous year's heavy cropping, animal or windstorm damage) had very few fruit in the following year the nuts themselves grew larger. The likely conclusion was that this was due to the thinned-out foliage and reduced number of shoots. The removal of dead wood in otherwise unpruned trees would have indicated that a large percentage of limbs and twigs under the constant heavy shade of the canopy died out or were so weakened as to become unproductive. Thus the idea was fostered of producing a spreading or vase-shaped tree, open in the centre to allow extra light to penetrate and to initiate fruit-producing spurs along the lower limbs within the tree. Many variations of this vase system were developed for use in commercial orchards, although in the past most nut trees were left virtually unpruned because many were grown only as trees in shelter belts.

Many types of nut trees grow very strongly and reach a huge size when pruned by the open vase or central leader system; this is why trees in old orchard plantings were often given as much as 4–8 m radial space all around each tree.

Espalier pruning, a system of training strong-growing trees to spread against a wall by using special pruning techniques, was developed parallel with the vase pruning system. This enabled trees to grow in a sheltered area of limited size, and to protect them from extreme weather conditions in cool climates. Many tree nut species such as almonds and walnuts are now being grown close-spaced to dwarf the trees and obtain earlier cropping. Lychee trees (see next section) are being pruned constantly into low-growing, spreading trees so that they can be grown completely under cover. This trend is likely to spread to many other nut species, mainly to protect the trees and crops from weather and pest predation.

Pruning systems currently in use are described below, followed by an explanation of my own pruning system developed over many years of experimentation.

Vase shape: With this system 'rods' (trees with one single growth shoot) are purchased. After the tree is planted it is pruned severely to about knee height. This produces 3–4 branches by the following winter.

The tree is severely pruned again during the second winter, each branch being cut back to leave only 4–6 buds, picking two adjacent buds to form the next two limbs. The following summer these buds form shoots that grow to produce 8–12 branches, enough to form the foundation of the pruning system for most species of fruit trees. If more branches are needed another hard pruning is done during the third winter season.

High trunk: This system is ideal for small areas and for small gardens, when gardeners want to grow their fruit trees to maximise use of vertical space. To do this they allow the fruit trees to grow high trunks to about 4–5 m, using stakes for support. When the tree has reached the desired height they use either the vase or central leader pruning method. The only difference from the traditional vase system is that the tree shape is formed well above the ground to allow full use of the area under the tree. This system is also used in permaculture where gardeners or small farmers want to run animals or to grow other crops around the nut trees, or to provide some shelter for plants and animals.

Central leader pruning: This system was developed to produce pyramid-shaped trees. The rod or single trunk tree purchased from the nursery is planted without any pruning. This tree grows as a single leader tree, developing a natural spiral of almost horizontal branches that are

Pyramid-shaped almond tree (*Prunus dulcis*) with two centre branches removed to make an open vase-shaped tree

rarely pruned, but are often trained with pieces of wire or pegs to form a wide-angled crotch (of 30–35°) where the branch joins the main trunk for strengthening.

Branches that start to grow immediately under or crowd another limb are removed so that the limbs form an open spiral pattern. The top shoot is allowed to continue to grow as a single trunk; competing branches within 30cm of the top shoot are removed. Thinning of the spur systems (which have developed on all limbs of the tree) may be needed every now and then, but very little overall pruning is necessary for the life of the tree. Some propping of branches with a 'Y'-shaped pole or support may be needed when the tree has heavy crops of nuts.

Modified central leader: This system has all the limbs except the central one tip-pruned to promote extra fruiting wood.

Delayed vase: Such a system can be produced from a central leader tree by removing the central growth to about 1–2 m from the ground after 5–9 years of being trained as a central leader. This method is being used very successfully for chestnut trees, almonds and walnuts.

Espalier training of nut trees

When the Persians conquered the Egyptians in 525 BC, their landscape design was changed by contact with Egyptian walled gardens, which the conquerors adopted and developed for themselves. Within these garden walls, space was at a premium, and the need to accommodate fruit trees, an essential part of Persian garden design, led to the development of wall-training methods. These same espalier training systems were adopted later by French and English gardeners between the fifteenth and eighteenth centuries, becoming the traditional method of managing trees under cover in glasshouses. In very cold areas, fruit crops that flower early, such as almonds, could only be grown under glass or in a sheltered place to protect the trees from late, early or mid-season frosts.

All espalier methods entail pruning and training branches to create a particular design shape and to make fruiting spur systems grow evenly along each entire branch, enabling maximum cropping all over the tree.

There are a great number of intriguing espalier design shapes: flattened fan; flattened multiple T; candelabrum; flattened multiple candelabrum (palmate); flattened multiple Y; cordons (one limb only bent at a slight angle); cordons cross-pleached to form a flat living fence; umbrella (with high trunk); T umbrella (e.g. Lincoln trellis) with spreading limbs to form a canopy; flattened spreading multiple Y; and all the above with various pleaching (joining limbs by grafting), hollow pyramids, hollow flat-sided pyramids, and various trellis designs, including the New Zealand designed EBRO™ system, and arbour covering patterns. Most of the designs I have seen in Australia are of the multiple T, candelabra, cordon or multiple Y shape. The most suitable shape for almond trees is an open fan shape.

Fan shaped espalier: Trees bought from a nursery that are to be trained into a fan shape have some limbs removed so that the limbs left on the tree are in the one vertical plane. This allows the branches to grow in a flattened position against a fence, frame or trellis. After the tree is planted, fertilised, watered and if necessary staked, the branches are pulled apart into a fan shape like the fingers of a hand. Each limb can be tied into place, preferably with material such as strips of cloth sheeting or perishable rubber, as these will not restrict the limb growth if they are accidentally left in place. The limbs are lightly pruned and will, with luck, produce some nuts in the first year although usually a wait of 3–5 years is normal. An alternative to leaving the tree unpruned is to cut each of the 4–5 limbs back to a 10 cm stump to produce more limbs in a fan shape ready to be trained the following year.

Prunus dulcis 'All in One' almond tree beginning to flower. Tree has been trained as a fan-shaped espalier.

Almond (*Prunus dulcis*) tree limb, spur pruned, a system that is not in favour.

The maximum number of limbs for a fan shape will depend on the space given for it to grow but 10–20 limbs are suggested as a guide. Every season more strong growths will grow from the original limbs and these can be incorporated into the design or the older branches cut back to the new more healthy shoots and these in turn tied into place. Almonds can be spur pruned but perform just as well with just a little 'chunk' pruning (see Glossary).

With the trend towards small gardens, space saving, patio gardens and gardening in units and flats, the concept of espalier gardening is becoming more and more popular. A point of interest is that only one tree is needed if gardeners graft another cross-pollinating almond cultivar (or several) onto the one tree (see the chapter on budding and grafting). The beauty of a multiple-grafted espalier tree is that pollination is guaranteed and a gardener could eventually be picking a selection of fruit of different cultivars from the one tree.

While espalier pruning uses some of the same techniques as other pruning systems, certain special systems have been developed which can be adopted for other nut tree species. Gardeners can employ partial cincturing (placing a cut above a bud) or notching (a notch of wood cut out above a bud) to initiate spur or shoot growth on a bare part of a limb. Cincturing around the whole branch is also used to promote fruiting (see Glossary).

A new concept of summer pruning

I first saw reference to summer pruning in a book by George Quinn, *Fruit Tree and Grape Vine Pruning: A handbook for fruit and vine growers*, first published in 1913. Quinn was a horticultural instructor with the South Australian Department of Agriculture and he mentions summer pruning as a method of shaping young trees and for removing shading branches. He discusses the effect of summer pruning and partially broken branches on bud formation, mainly dealing with young trees. I have developed this idea and used summer pruning trees and espalier systems to reduce the amount of pruning needed each year and to obtain better flower bud formation on spurs.

My own experimentation with various deciduous fruit trees has shown that partial late-summer pruning (the bending of laterals so that they break almost in half but are left hanging on the tree) is an effective way to reduce overall pruning needs. This method has been used on hazelnuts and walnuts and should work with many of the other nut tree species. It has the advantage of aiding the formation of more spurs than the traditional method of continuous pruning. To achieve best results, the bending of shoots should be done only once, in the December or early January period or when the spring–summer growth had ceased.

If this bending is done too early the shoots will just multiply and not form many fruiting spurs. When bending the shoots, I recommend placing the bend at the point where a 5cm stub is left; this is usually where the fifth to eighth mature leaf occurs on the shoot. The spurs will form on that short stub section nearest the main limb, allowing pruning back to those spurs during the following winter.

One disadvantage of the bent-shoot summer pruning method is that the shoots all hang down and look untidy, and many will partially die. While some gardeners dislike this untidy look the results and the time saved make it worthwhile. Once the tree has settled down and created many spur systems, there will be less total growth on the tree during the summer period, thus requiring less pruning or bending of the laterals.

My own pruning system

I have developed my own pruning system over a period of about 20 years. It is a new approach and is suitable for most deciduous fruit trees except peaches and nectarines. It is also suitable for nut trees that usually grow into large specimens when left unpruned.

Almond tree
(*Prunus dulcis*)
being retrained
using the author's
new pruning
technique.

Old seedling
walnut tree pruned
three times to
achieve multiple
branching.

Same seedling, the
following April,
showing resultant
low growth habit and
large crop of walnuts

This new system is somewhat contradictory because, although the initial tree shaping stage requires very, very severe pruning of young trees, once the tree shape is formed only maintenance pruning is needed. Although this method is best begun on young trees in order to obtain better shapes, mature trees and any trees currently pruned to conventional open vase shapes or central leader systems can be easily changed to this new system.

I first tried this method on apples, plums and pears and it worked wonderfully. Since then I have used the system on walnuts and almonds and I have seen cashew nut trees treated in the same way.

The system involves the same steps as does that of the vase shape, pruning the tree very hard in the first year, then up until about year three depending upon tree vigour and whether summer pruning is done. If gardeners choose a well-rooted multi-branched tree from the plant nursery then they will be in front and have 4–6 branches already developed.

It is normal practice to prune young trees back to short branch stubs in their first year after purchase from a garden centre or plant nursery. Many home gardeners are too frightened to prune young trees hard and only tip prune by removing 10–20 cm of growth from each branch. Tip pruning is not acceptable for young trees, no matter what system of pruning is to be adopted because the trees will become tall and leggy. Trees purchased from nurseries usually have from three to five branches already formed on them. Young trees should have any branches growing directly up the centre of the tree removed completely. If left they tend to become dominant. All other branches can be cut back to leave 5–6 buds (or leaves) on each stub. The two top-most buds on each stub should face to the side of the branch. Any buds facing into the centre of the tree should be cut off with a sharp knife, or by using the blade of sharp secateurs, to prevent branches growing into the centre of the tree.

Most pruners prune deciduous trees just once a year in winter. If this method is used it will take about four years to form the desired number of branches for the new system, but may be less with evergreen nut tree species as they are growing for a longer period. If summer pruning is used at a time when the new shoots on the branches are 10–20 cm long (November–December period), then the number of branches will double. All that is required is to cut the shoots off evenly like a crew-cut and to leave about four to five leaves on each stub. This causes the branch to grow at least two more shoots from the cut ends of the branches. With very vigorous trees, this summer pruning can be done twice so as to triple the number of branches formed in one season.

A young tree with four original branches pruned in winter will produce about eight branches by the following winter season. If the same tree is summer pruned it will produce about 16 branches and if summer pruned twice will produce about 32 branches by the following autumn. Note that evergreen trees or shrubs are usually pruned just before a growth surge or during early spring. To make sure that the trees grow strongly, and to enable them to withstand two summer prunings, it is necessary to keep watering and fertilising them. The soil must be kept moist but not wet; the trees must not be allowed to become dust-dry. Fertiliser should be applied regularly every month during the growing season from early spring to mid-summer, but at a much reduced rate than that recommended for mature trees.

If the fruit tree is summer pruned once and has about 16 branches on it by the following pruning period, then these main branches are again pruned back to 4–5 buds so as to double up the number of branches (to about 30) formed on the tree during the following season. Summer pruning of trees with this number of growing branches is not necessary; they are just left to grow naturally for one year. By the next pruning the tree will have grown about 30 strong branches evenly spaced around the vase shaped base of the tree. The branches will have grown very strongly and may reach 2–4 m in length, especially with some nut species.

The diversion from other pruning systems begins at the point when the required number of branches has grown. It is important not to prune any material from the branches at this stage. Apart from removing crossing branches, dead wood and watershoots in the centre of the tree, none of the branches are pruned and gardeners must resist the temptation to even tip prune the long, often whippy, bent branches, some of which could be 5–6 m long. These young branches left unpruned will develop short growths (spurs and short fruiting laterals) all along the unpruned limbs. If a branch is tipped or cut, strong growth will occur from the end of that branch and hardly any spur growth will form along it. With most species, even if 1–2 cm are pruned from the top of any one branch, this pruning will prevent the formation of evenly spaced spurs along its length. The branch will revert to forming strong top growth and very few spurs, with the result that it will have large bare sections containing no spurs. Do not worry about crossing or tangled branches; leave them in place to produce fruit — they can be shortened at a later stage if necessary. The small laterals on the tree should not be pruned at this stage but left to form fruiting spurs.

Each spur site produces a bunch of leaves and the foliage thus created can be likened to a tube of shoots and leaves along each branch. Because the leaves are formed in this fashion more light gets into the centre and to the base of the tree. The effect is that the bottom branches and laterals remain healthy and fruitful and do not die out through lack of light. Vase shape or central leader pruning systems usually result in the tree losing lateral and spur vigour in the centre and lower area because of the thick upper foliage that develops and gives too much shade inside the tree. This factor is relevant to many nut tree species.

The fruiting spurs that are formed in the first year of non-pruning will produce fruits the following year. The second year of non-pruning is the formative year for the tree. The thin, whippy young branches, unable to hold the weight of fruit, will bend downwards and the tree will take on a weeping, mushroom shape which reduces its size and brings it to an easily managed level. Once a branch has been bent into a shape for about eight months it will stay bent. It may be necessary to place props under some of the heavily laden branches to prevent their breaking. Thinning the nuts will also reduce the weight on branches, but this operation is usually not needed. Weights can be placed on any stiff upright limbs at this stage to aid in the bending process if necessary.

Once the tree shape has formed after the two non-pruning years, subsequent pruning is minimal: broken branches are cut off, thick spur systems are thinned and the odd branch is cut out to reduce overcrowding. Any new laterals or branches that grow are left unpruned and they will then spur up, produce fruit and become weeping parts of the tree. About every five years the tree will need some of the spreading sideway branches trimmed back and the whole tree thinned a little with 'chunk' pruning — pruning random pieces from the spurs and sections of the tree. This operation will need about 10–50 cuts only, very few secateur cuts compared to conventional systems where winter pruning of a tree the same age would need up to 1–2000 cuts or even more.

One of the aims of this new pruning system is to let the tree produce nuts as early as possible. Early fruiting actually has a dwarfing effect: the tree goes into 'fruiting mode' and all its energy is given to the production of nuts instead of long, strong lateral growths and watershoots.

Trees pruned to this method spread out sideways instead of upwards, but remain at picking height from the ground. They have nuts every year and the problem of biennial bearing disappears. The trees need very little maintenance. Light is allowed into all parts of the tree so that nuts are produced in the centre and to ground level. When the tree is dwarfed, it makes spraying, picking and pruning a lightweight job and netting of the orchard is easier. This pruning system can be used for pot-grown plants, and creates a low, spreading, early fruiting tree that is very easily managed.

Other

NUTS

Bunya Bunya pine

Araucaria bidwillii

The Bunya Bunya pine (family *Araucariaceae*) belongs to a group of plants containing only 18 species. These related species include the popular Norfolk Island pine (*Araucaria heterophylla*) and the monkey puzzle tree (*A. araucana*). The Bunya Bunya pine is a giant tree, native to Queensland and usually found growing in areas of rainforest. The branches are whorled and the small, leathery, spiky leaves are closely gathered to these branches.

The Bunya Bunya pine will grow to about 45 m tall, but only where it receives warmth and is free of heavy frosts, so it is often used in coastal plantings. Despite being a warm climate plant it will grow successfully as far south as Melbourne where it features in many large gardens and parkland areas. The trees are not a forest forming species but grow separately as individuals within the rainforests of Queensland.

The Bunya Bunya pine is propagated by fresh seed obtained from the giant cones that fall. Young trees should be protected from heavy frosts; staking may be necessary but no pruning is needed as this will spoil the natural shape of the tree.

Male and female cones are formed on the one tree or may be on separate

Bunya Bunya pine
(*Araucaria bidwillii*)
seed cone held by
Alexandria Volkov

trees. The nuts are in the huge female cones which may take 2–3 years to mature; individual cones can weigh 5 kg or more and are shed from the tree when mature. Because of this natural cone shedding it is wise to stay away from trees when the dropping period begins. One cone dropped from 30 m or more could easily crush one's skull.

The nuts are eaten raw or can be roasted and are very nutritious and tasty. Traditionally Australian Aboriginal peoples used to travel long distances to where small groups of Bunya Bunya pine were growing to join in festivals especially conducted to celebrate the harvesting of the nuts. These nuts are now being sought after by native food collectors for use in restaurants that serve natural Australian foodstuffs and devise recipes.

ROASTED BUNYA NUTS

Remove pointed end of bunya nut. Dry roast as for chestnuts at 180°C for approximately 40 minutes.

(Chinese) Lychee nuts
Litchi chinensis

The lychee plant belongs to the *Sapindaceae* (soap berry) family, which also contains many species that provide other edible fruits such as the akee (*Blighia sapida*), the rambutan (*Nephelium lappaceum*) and the longan (*Euporia longan*). In the same family, there are also some popular ornamental plants such as the tulipwood tree (*Harpullia pendula*) and the golden-rain tree (*Kolreuteria formosana*).

The lychee is a tropical to semi-tropical tree that can grow as tall as 14 m. Commercial cultivars of lychees usually develop into spreading trees with foliage extending to the ground. Lychees are grown commercially in Australia, in parts of North and South America, India and in some countries of South-East Asia.

Lychee trees have pinnate leaves (that is the leaves have many leaflets), which are leathery, dark green on the surface, and are an elliptical, pointed shape. Young leaves are a deep reddish colour before maturity. Both male and female flowers occur in a large inflorescence. The fruit that are formed are single-seeded with a red, yellowish or pink bubbly-surfaced 'shell' lined with a fleshy substance (aril) around a white seed that is almost transparent and very edible. As the flowers are borne at the foliage tips the fruit can be seen hanging in colourful bunches outside the tree canopy which makes them easier to harvest.

The first fruits to arrive in Australia were probably in the dried form sold as lychee nuts, although some plants were grown from imported seeds soon after Australia was colonised during the early 1800s. Although not a true nut (botanically), the dried fruits of the lychee are often called 'lychee nuts' and are sold as such in market places and in Chinese food shops.

Care and maintenance

Lychee var. 'Bengal', South-East Queensland

Lychee trees are grown in tropical to semi-tropical climates and, in Australia, as far south as Mildura in Victoria in a protected greenhouse. They require well-drained soils but are not too fussy otherwise, provided they do not become waterlogged. They are, however, very specific in their climatic requirements. For maximum growth they need very high humidity and rainfall associated with warm weather conditions, but still need a dry period during fruiting in autumn and a cool period during the autumn to early winter phase. A vegetative dormancy period is necessary for flowering; the cool period should not get below 8°C as this may impede flower opening.

Watering is needed from fruit set to harvest and young trees need constant watering for maximum vegetative growth. The trees benefit from several applications of a complete or general organic fertiliser containing high nitrogen, low phosphorous and high potassium (NPK).

Lychee trees are not generally pruned for shaping, except when young, but many commercial growers prune just after harvest to promote more laterals: this will give better crops because the plant fruits on new growth. Because these plants are subject to flying fox damage early pruning to produce many-branched, low-growing trees, easily netted, is recommended.

Care must also be taken when planting young trees because they have tender roots.

Propagation

Most lychee trees are propagated by 'marcotting', a form of layering that involves taking off bark from the limb of a tree, then wrapping a material such as moist sphagnum moss around this area and enclosing the whole lot in plastic or aluminium foil to seal it. Roots grow from the wound area into the moss, then the branch is severed and placed into a pot. (see Propagation chapter)

Grafting and budding can be used for propagation although the success rate is not great.

Lychees will also grow from cuttings but do not seem to establish as well as the marcotted material.

Pests and diseases

There are many pests and diseases that attack lychee trees including the macadamia nut borer, stem girdlers, moths, scale insects, erinose mites and flying foxes (bats).

There are organic as well as chemical methods to control most insect pests and diseases but netting seems to be the only method to prevent flying foxes creating havoc.

Harvesting and storage

The lychees are harvested over about a three-week period in autumn when the fruit have developed full flavour. Fresh fruits will store for few weeks in cool storage at 5°C but most fruits are eaten fresh from the tree. Whole fruits may be frozen. Shelled lychee fruits have also been processed and canned and whole fruits dried.

Fruits must be dried to produce the lychee nuts, but then they lose their fantastic red–pink shell colour. The white flesh inside shrinks, leaving a gap between the outer shell and the inside seed and flesh. The flesh turns a brownish colour not unlike dates and is a good substitute when fresh fruits are unavailable.

Some of the cultivars that are being grown in Australia include Bengal, Bosworth 3, Gee Chee, Haak Yip, Kwai May Pink, Salathial, Tai So, Wai Chee.

Ginkgo nuts

Ginkgo biloba

The ginkgo tree is an ancient deciduous tree that once covered a large area of the planet. At one stage it was thought to be extinct but in 1691 a German botanist, Engelbert Kaempfer, rediscovered it growing in China where it had been and still is revered as a sacred tree. Even today large trees over 1000 years old can be seen growing in some Chinese Buddhist shrine sites. Some of the older trees develop callused growth in the bark of the trunk which looks like folds of skin. This attractive feature can take a very long time to develop.

The ginkgo is the only living member of the order of plants known as Gingkoales, and the only remaining member of the plant family *Gingkoaceae*, so can truly be regarded as a living fossil. Fossil remains indicate that at one time, about 140 million yeara ago, there would have been ginkgo trees over many parts of the earth. The gingko is now thought to be completely extinct in the wild. It has, however, been successfully propagated and is now grown in many parts of the world. There are specimens in just about every botanical garden and arboretum around the world.

The genus name ginkgo comes from the Chinese word 'ginkyo' meaning 'silver apricot' and the species name *biloba* means 'two-lobed'. The name *Gingko biloba* was given by Linnaeus, the great plant classifier, although it was also given another name *Salisburia adiantifolia* by an English botanist, Smith, and this name remains a synonym. The gingko has some unique features: it is more like a conifer than a broadleaf tree but it is deciduous; it is like a fern in some ways but is not a fern either; it has some similarities to the cycads; it is the only living seed-producing plant to have free-swimming sperm

This tree does not have what is described as true leaves (i.e. leaves with a main central vein with defined veins forking out from this). Ginkgo leaves are leathery, fan-shaped and bilobed, with a long stem and radiating veins of equal size. The ginkgo is also known as the maiden-hair tree as the foliage, although much larger, is the same shape as leaflets of the maiden-hair fern. In fact, the leaf shape can be likened to a duck or waterfowl's webbed foot and this has given the tree its common name

in China, of duck's foot tree. The tree's autumn foliage is spectacular, turning a brilliant canary yellow in good autumn weather conditions.

The ginkgo has separate male and female trees and the male form is commonly grown in gardens for its pyramid shape and beautiful autumn foliage. It can grow as high as 40 m with a spread of up to 9 m, so it needs plenty of space. Female trees bear fruits that produce seeds, the kernels of which, once fertilised, can be eaten as nuts. Unfortunately, this fruit has a very, very unpleasant smell and this is why they are generally not grown in gardens.

Care and maintenance

The gingko tree can live to an age of 1000 years. The oldest gingko in China is said to be over 3500 years old. Gingko trees require little maintenance. They will grow in many types of soil providing it is deep and well drained. The trees retain their pyramid shape for many years until in old age they develop growth similar to other trees with rounded tops. Being deciduous they need some cold weather during the autumn–winter period and can look great when grown in small copses.

The trees need little pruning, but if they do it should be done in spring and while they are young. Gingko trees can also be grown successfully as bonsai.

Ginkgo tree
(*Ginkgo biloba*)
autumn foliage

Propagation

Male forms of this tree are readily available from plant nurseries; female forms may be more difficult to find but seedlings will produce both male and female forms.

Ginkgo trees can be easily propagated by seed and will also grow from hardwood cuttings taken in winter. In late summer, the seeds can be collected and cleaned of all flesh, then planted immediately or stored in material such as damp sand and given a vernalisation period (cool temperature such as provided by placing the seeds and container in the refrigerator for a few weeks) before sowing in spring. For the production of nuts it is necessary to grow both the male and female trees for pollination purposes.

Pests and diseases

The gingko is a hardy tree and resistant to most pests and diseases. It seems to resist pollution and so is often planted as a street tree. The tree also seems able to withstand the effects of snow, ice and frost and to adapt to changes in levels of carbon dioxide so can cope with the greenhouse effect.

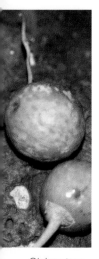

Ginkgo tree
(*Ginkgo biloba*)
Collected, fallen
fruits from
female tree

Harvesting and use of nuts

The seeds, which generally fall to the ground after leaf fall in autumn, are encased in a fleshy outer covering that smells like rancid butter as it rots. All fruit collected must be thoroughly cleaned of every vestige of flesh because of its obnoxious smell. This should be done carefully while wearing rubber gloves for protection against the butyric acid in the flesh which can cause a dermatitis-like condition in some people. The seed coat also contains a substance similar to that found in poison ivy and this may also cause irritation. After the flesh is cleaned off in water, the seeds should be thoroughly washed and dried. The nuts can then be boiled or roasted and salted.

Once prepared, ginkgo nuts look similar to pistachio nuts. When the shell is partially split the nuts are easily opened to obtain the kernel inside. They are very nutritious and have many uses in traditional Chinese medicine. They are said to aid digestion, and to help expel intestestinal worms. The nuts can be bought loose in bags in China, often roasted and salted. (I found that once I started eating them I just wanted to eat more and more.) Canned nuts are also available in China and are used in stews and stir fries and as an addition to other meals.

Ginkgo nuts are an ingredient in the popular Japanese dish *chawan mushi*, or savoury cup custard, where they are used whole, peeled and shelled They turn a pale green when cooked and have a mild, slightly nutty flavour. They are also eaten skewered and grilled.

Young fruits have also been used to treat tuberculosis and the pulp from ripe fruits is said to have been used for ailments such as asthma, kidney and bladder problems, coughs and even gonorrhoea.

Extract of the leaves of *Gingko biloba* have been adopted by Western medicine for use in many preparations, but has been used for centuries by the Chinese. The leaves themselves were often placed between the pages of treasured books to protect them from insect predation. *Gingko biloba* is sold in Western countries as a herbal supplement to enhance memory and improve mental clarity, as an antioxidant and for its contribution to the health of the cardiovascular and nervous systems.

Indian almond (*Terminalia catappa*) showing one leaf, green and ripe fruits, and some fruits damaged by flying foxes, Cairns, Qld.

(Indian) Almonds

Terminalia catappa

The India almond tree (family *Combretaceae*) is a tropical deciduous tree with large leaves from 10–33 cm long. In Australia, the Indian almond can be found growing in the Northern Territory and North East Queensland to the Torres Strait. The tree is also found in Polynesia and the South-East Asian region. Other species of *Terminalia* can also be found growing in Queensland and the Northern Territory; these include: *T. arostrata, T. carpentariae, T. erythrocarpa, T. ferdinandiana, T. grandiflora, T. pterocarya*, but not all have edible nuts.

These trees can grow to 15 m and are found in many countries along the seashore where it is thought seeds have lodged after being carried by sea currents. The tree has horizontal tiered branches, and the leaves are an oval shape and glossy green. The slightly scented flowers are insignificant and are in spikes a the ends of branches.

The trees need well-drained soils and a sunny position and can withstand salt air conditions.

The Indian almond produces fruits that look like almond fruits (*Prunus amygdalus*) if viewed on their side as they have a suture line in the fleshy

seed coating that runs the length of the fruit. The shell is oval shaped with flattened edges and the kernels contain a high percentage of oil. They are eaten raw or roasted. Parts of this tree have been used for tanning and the leaves can be used to feed silkworms.

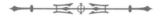

Peanuts

Arachis hypogaea

Peanuts are not true nuts in botanical terms but are regarded as such by all who consume these delectable underground seeds or 'earth nuts'. The common peanut, now taken for granted in most cultures, is produced on a plant belonging to the legume family (*Leguminosae*) and its place of origin is South America. The peanut is probably one of the most widely used nuts in the world today.

Peanuts are now grown commercially in many countries including

Australia, Argentina, China, India and the USA. In China peanuts are seen everywhere in the market places and are used to produce a plethora of sweets and foodstuffs as well as being included in many stir-fried meals. Peanut oil is used for cooking. The pressed material left from the extraction of oil is known as peanut cake and is used for animal feed and as a fertiliser.

Peanuts have been grown in Australia since the late 19th century, and the plant is thought to have been introduced by Chinese gold fossickers. In the 1921, WA Department of Agriculture's *Handbook of Horticulture and Viticulture of Western Australia*, peanuts are described as being a crop worth considering for growing in that state. The processing stages of the peanut are described thus: 'The nuts are graded, stacked, and sold in large quantities for eating, while an enormous amount is crushed in mills, where the oil — of which the nut contains over 40% — is extracted, and the residue compressed and sold for feeding stock. The oil, which is largely used for lighting and soap making, is imported into Australia in large quantities.' (p. 300)

The description continues: 'The nuts are bought by the shipload from the Levant and from India and treated in the large olive oil mills around Marseilles. The nuts are first crushed and cold pressed, yielding an almost colourless oil, of pleasant taste and smell, which is used as an adulterant of salad oil. It is easily extracted, does not readily turn rancid and is palatable. The paste is then sprinkled with water and pressed again, cold, the oil being used mostly for lighting. The third oil is next extracted from the steamed paste, and is in great demand for soap making, while the residue cake constitutes excellent food for stock, being palatable,

Courtesy Ian Crosthwaite

Pegs from the base of the flower penetrate the soil where the peanut is formed.

Peanut (*Arachis hypogaea*) for sale, open market place, Chengdu, China

rich in protein and in starchy and sugary matters, apart from the unextracted percentage of oil remaining in the residue.' (p. 300)

The peanut plant is a legume (it can produce its own nitrogen supply from nodules made by bacteria living on its roots). Individual plants can grow to about 0.5 m tall and have a spreading habit with a deep taproot system. The plants look a little like the common field clover. They have the same type of leaf structure although there are usually four leaflets forming each entire leaf instead of the clover's three and they have tiny, yellow, pea-like flowers. Some types have a creeping sprawling growth habit, while others are more upright. Some cultivars produce large nuts, some small.

Peanut plants differ from other species in the same family in that the flowers, once fertilised, begin to form a 'peg', the flower stem elongates and allows the 'peg' to penetrate the loose soil surrounding the plant. This 'peg' enlarges and forms the peanut which is the seed of the plant. The peanut plant needs sandy or very loose fertile soils in which to grow successfully and must have fairly high temperatures, so it is most suited to semi-tropical and tropical areas. Plants require a long 'frost free' growth period of about five months because the plant is very susceptible to frost and cold damage.

Peanuts can be grown in more southerly areas in Australia; I have seen peanuts grown in a home garden in central Victoria during the warm summer months.

Care and maintenance

The nuts are sown into soil that has had some lime added in the form of gypsum. Gypsum is often preferred because it also supplies sulphur.

Peanut plants require all major nutrients (nitrogen, phosphorous, potassium) for good growth but do also need sulphur and magnesium for quality nut production. Calcium is essential for nut (kernel) formation. When planting, the seeds (peanuts) are spaced to give up to 10 or more plants per metre and are placed about 50 mm deep. Some gardeners crack the seed shell before planting to allow for easy germination. Good weed control practices are essential, together with keeping the soil surrounding the plants loose and friable until plants spread and grow together.

EASY SATAY PEANUT SAUCE

Fry finely chopped onion in a little oil until transparent. Add 3/4 cup peanut butter, 3/4 cup water, 2 tsp soy sauce, 1/2 tsp honey, 1 tsp dried chilli. Simmer 3 minutes. Mix in 1/2 cup crushed mixed nuts and serve hot.

BANANA SPREAD

3 ripe mashed bananas

1 1/2 tsp each cinnamon, sesame seeds, honey and lemon juice together with 1/2 cup crushed peanuts (or crushed mixed nuts) and 1/2 cup sultanas. Use in sandwiches.

Propagation

Because this plant is an annual it has to be propagated by seed each season. The seeds used are the raw 'peanuts' that we eat. Some growers extract the kernels from the nuts before sowing, others plant the whole peanut, shell and all. They are planted about half a metre apart at a depth of about 2–3 cm. They can be sown in pots or in row formation in the soil or they can be used as a cover crop in the garden. It is very important to keep weeds at bay and to have the soil 'tilth' at such a consistency that allows easy emergence of the germinating seeds.

Pests and diseases

Peanut plants are subject to many pests and diseases but generally these have no serious effects. Sometimes sucking insect such as jassids may occur in plague proportions, and during some seasons cut worms and army worms eat the leaves of plants and cause problems especially to seedling plants. Soil-inhabiting larvae, including cane grubs, white fringed weevil larvae and false wireworms, can attack plants, especially the roots and developing nuts. Leaf spot, net blotch and rust may infect leaves and many soil-borne diseases such as Cylindrocladium Black Rot, sclerotinia and white mould can infect peanut plants.

By spraying organic materials or chemicals for pests or diseases only when it is absolutely essential to do so and by using crop rotation methods, good weed control, adequate watering and fertiliser applications, pest and disease problems can be minimised.

Harvesting and use

Peanuts start to mature when plants begin to dry and become scraggly at the end of the summer season. At this stage they can be gently lifted with a multi-pronged fork so that the peanuts are not cut or removed accidentally. Once the plants are uprooted they can be left in the sun with the nuts exposed until the plant wilts. The soil is then removed from around the roots and the nuts left to dry for a few weeks more. They are then picked off the plant and stored in a dry place.

Commercially, peanuts are harvested by uprooting and pushing the plants into rows with a special combine machine. The whole row of plants is then inverted to allow better drying and when their moisture content is about 13% they can be collected for storage. Growers with access to dryers can collect the peanuts when the pod moisture content is 18–20%, thresh them and take them to a dryer.

Harvested nuts are graded, with different sized nuts used for different purposes. Large nuts mostly supply snack food markets whilst others are crushed for oil.

Peanuts can be eaten raw or roasted. The most common product is salted and unsalted roasted peanuts.

Peanuts contain lipids (fats and oils), some of the essential amino acids, are full of calories, carbohydrates and protein, and provide some major and minor nutrients such as calcium, phosphorous, potassium, sodium, iron, magnesium, copper, and manganese. Peanuts also yield small amounts of vitamin E and the B group of vitamins B2, B3, B5, B6 biotin and folic acid.

Most of the world's vegetable oil comes either from peanuts or soya beans. Cold pressed peanut oil contains about 80% unsaturated lipids and 20% saturated.

Peanut butter is another major use of peanuts. It was patented in the United States in 1890 by a St Louis doctor, and was first promoted at the St Louis World Fair in 1904. While it was originally intended as a protein substitute for people whose bad teeth prevented their chewing meat, it received greater endorsement from young people and went on to become seen as the all-American biscuit and toast accompaniment The first branded version was Skippy Peanut Butter developed by the Rosefield Packing Company of Alameda in California.

A small percentage of humans are allergic to peanuts and may show mild or even severe allergy reaction, so it is essential to make sure that visitors know when peanut products are being used to prepare food in your house. Some schools in America have banned the sale of peanut butter and peanuts because of the risk of anaphylactic allergy reactions. Symptoms vary from mild irriation or skin blemishes to swelling of internal organs, redness of face, shock and difficulty in breathing, which can become life threatening. Work is being done to breed or produce allergy-free peanuts to overcome this problem.

Pine nuts

Pinus   spp.

Pine nuts or pinons are produced in the seed-bearing cone of coni-fers from the *Pinus* species of plants (family *Taxodiaceae*). Humans have been harvesting pine nuts as a source of food for centuries, and there is evidence of their use found in ancient cave sites. Pine nuts were originally collected from virgin forest areas, but now most are grown commercially.

The *Pinus* species are trees with spiky, round, needle-like leaves in clusters and many make good timber trees. A number of the pine nut trees are slow growing but do, over time, reach very large proportions. They make very good wind breaks, can be planted for timber or be used singly as a specimen tree in a landscape feature. They are salt tolerant and are often found planted near the coastline.

Those *Pinus* species that do not have large seeds in the cones are not used to produce pine nuts: it would be uneconomical to collect them, so the larger nuts produced by others can, in their way, be considered a bonus.

Some of the species that produce usable pine nuts include *Pinus mono-phylla,* used by American Indians as a food source for thousands of years, the Colorado pinon (*P. edulis*), also used by American Indians and now an important source of pine nuts in America, and the Mexican pinon (*P. cembroides*). European pine nuts include the Italian stone pine (*P. pinea*), and the Swiss stone pine(*P. cembra*). Other edible pine nuts include *P. siburica*, which grows in Russia, *P. koraiensis* from Korea, and *P. gerardiana*, native to the Himalayan region. There are many other *Pinus* species used throughout the world wherever they produce large edible nuts (seeds).

The Italian stone pine (*Pinus pinea*), the most common pine tree that produces nuts, grows in huge forest areas in Italy, Spain and Anatolia and it is here that most of the world supplies of pine nuts are harvested. There are, at present, no large commercial plantations in Australia.

Care and maintenance

The stone pine can grow up to 35 m tall in its natural environment but in most gardens may be smaller. The species is drought resistant and can tolerate many soil conditions, but not waterlogging. The stone pine has the typical conical growth habit of pines but once the tree is mature it spreads out into a flat-topped umbrella-shaped crown. Stone pines grown from seed will start producing small crops between the eighth and fifteenth years, then steadily improve cropping.

Pine nut (*Pinus pinea*) cone and seeds

To keep trees small, an option is to prune seedlings to make them branch at an early growth stage. Pine trees cannot be pruned into old wood as they will not resprout, but if the soft new growth shoots are clipped then these shoots will produce extra branches.

Propagation

Stone pines are readily propagated by seed, although seedlings can be grafted if a selected cultivar is needed. Seed collected and placed in a well-drained propagation mix in a cool place will germinate in the following season. To make sure the seed gets a vernalisation or cool temperature period (see Glossary) the seed can be stratified (i.e. placed in layers, see Glossary) in damp sand and put in a household refrigerator in the crisper section for a few weeks before planting the seed in spring. Grafted plants will produce cones within the first 3-4 years of growth.

Grafting of conifers (this includes *Pinus* spp.) has been done for many years and is usually caried out during autumn–winter period. The graft used most often is the side graft which retains the growth shoot of the rootstock plant until the scion has grafted properly. Wedge or cleft grafts have also been used on very young growing shoots particularly on those plants that have been developed in tissue culture. The only problem with grafting conifers is the growth shoot used for grafting has to be from the topmost part of the plant and if this is removed it can destroy the plants shape. Shoots taken from side branches will graft well but continue growing sideways instead of upwards.

DATE AND PINE NUT BALLS

125 g cream cheese
1 1/2 finely chopped dates
1/2 cup pine nuts chopped
Sesame seeds

Mix all together and form into small balls and roll in sesame seeds. Refrigerate until ready to serve. Serve with biscuits or as part of a fruit platter. Other nuts can be substitued for pine nuts for quite a different flavour.

Pests and disease

These particular pines, when grown in other countries, are attacked by few significant pests or diseases, and the cones are harvested before the release of the nuts so that animals such as squirrels do not get to many of them. Minimal pest and disease control measures for stone pines and conifers are also all that are needed in Australia, but cockatoos and large parrots may eat the immature cones and cause considerable damage to the crop.

Harvesting and use of nuts

The cones that produce the nuts take three years to mature on the tree. The pine nuts are the seeds that grow in pairs at the base of each 'scale' of the cone. Cones can be harvested in the fourth season, usually with long hooked poles. They are then dried in the sun to allow them to open and release the nuts. They are then threshed (either mechanically or by hand) to extract the nuts. Pine nuts are enclosed in a very hard shell that is usually covered in a black powdery substance, but they are relatively easily extracted. Kernels are very white and nutritious and have a large oil content (nearly 50%), so like other nuts need to be stored carefully in the refrigerator or freezer. They can be eaten raw or roasted and are often included in other food preparations to complement the meal. Pesto is a famous Italian pasta accompaniment made from pine nuts with basil and parmesan cheese.

Pine nuts are high in calories, carbohydrates and protein and also contain calcium, phosphorous, iron, vitamin A, and vitamins B1, B2, B3.

Some permaculture exponents have planted this tree as an extra food source and for shade.

A resin can also be collected by tapping the trunks.

Quandong
Santalum acuminatum

The quandong (family *Santalaceae*) is an Australian native plant that is only now being recognised as an orchard plant species of commercial value. The fruits of this plant (*Santalum acuminatum*) have been gathered by Aboriginal peoples for centuries and it was one of the first fruits to find favour with early settlers, who named it the native peach.

There are several species of quandong in Australia, including the bitter quandong (*Santalum. murrayannum*), of which the fruit and seed kernel are inedible, the northern sandalwood (*S. lanceolatum*) with small bluish edible fruits, and the sandalwood tree of commerce (*S. spicatum*), from which perfumed wood is obtained for carving and from which oil of sandalwood is also extracted.

Quandongs grow into small bushy trees and many have a distinctive weeping habit so are very attractive as ornamental garden plants. The quandong is a partially parasitic plant and needs another species from which to draw nourishment, especially during the period when it is establishing itself. It can sucker onto the roots of any plant that provides what it needs.

Care and maintenance

In the wild these trees grow in shale-type soils or where there are well drained sandy ridges. They are salt and low rainfall tolerant. They require little in the way of fertilisers and if any are given they must be organic and very low in phosphorous. Watering is needed after fruit set but as the plants are naturally fairly drought tolerant they can easily be overwatered.

Pruning is not usually needed as growers let the plant grow into a

Quandong (*Santalanum acuminatum*)

QUANDONG JAM

Quandong jam can be made in a similar way to other jams. I use equal weight of quandongs and sugar with very little liquid, although some recipes call for more water and more sugar.

1 kg fresh quandongs
1 kg sugar

Place sugar, quandongs in a large preserving pan with sufficient water to cover base of pan to no more than 1 cm. Place over low heat until sugar has dissolved, stirring constantly. Bring to boil then reduce heat enough to allow jam to maintain a constant steady boiling without boiling over or burning. Stir constantly. Cook until setting point is reached, then pour jam into sterilised jars and seal.

natural shape, but some early pruning will give more form to the quandong bush. An open cover (tree guard) will be an advantage to protect young plants from wind and animals. If plants are in the open sunlight some shade cloth cover will be an advantage while the plant is young.

Propagation

Because of the parasitism needs of the quandong, propagation has been difficult and it is only recently that there has been some success using a common grass species for the developing seedling to parasitise. However, the seeds can be germinated quite readily before being placed with a host plant.

Propagating the quandong plant can be done using uncracked nuts but one of the prblems has been the amount of bacterial and fungal organisms adhering to the shell surface or naturally occurring in soil mixes; these often infect the developing seedling or tend to cause the kernel to rot.

For best results it is necessary to crack open the 'nut', extract the seed and then clean it thoroughly with a bleach or antiseptic material before rinsing with pure, clean water. Put the seed in a sterile medium (steam if necessary) such as palm peat, pearlite or peat moss inside a plastic bag or in a pot and place the container in a warm, dark place. I have used a sealed plastic bag containing damp, but not wet, peat moss and placed the plant material in it with good results. Seed germination can also be assisted with the use of plant auxins (see Glossary) such as Gibberellic acid but these materials may not be readily available to home gardeners. Seeds (kernels) should germinate within 3–8 weeks of sowing and can then be transferred to pots. Whole seeds may take over one year to germinate as the seed coat has to break down and there may also be some seed germination inhibitors within the shell that prevent fast germination.

Once germinated the young plants are best transferred into a pot containing the root of another plant as a host. Couch grass and lucerne are two plants that have been used in pots containing the seedlings. The potting mix used should be low in phosphate as too much will kill the plant. The developing roots of the quandong are very sensitive and care must be taken when transferring the germinating seedling into the pot. The pots used to grow plants should be deep, not squat, as the roots of seedling are vigorous and grow deeply.

Once seedlings have developed they can be grafted with a selected scion cultivar but, because the stems of the plant are usually thin, some grafting methods are unsuitable. A side-graft, where the scion is poked into the side stem of a growing seedling, or a wedge (cleft) graft using defoliated scions (removal of leaves), can be used. With the wedge graft, stretch plastic such as 'Parafilm' is used to wrap around the whole graft area or, alternatively, all the scion should be covered with the wrap. The trick for success is to use a sealed plastic sleeve over the scion piece to prevent it drying out. Some water can be squirted into the plastic sleeve to provide humidity (see also pp. 71–85 on grafting). My own system (although not yet tried with quangdongs) of using a plastic sleeve and scions with leaves still attached may be worth trying (see Grafting section). Grafted plants can be planted out into the field as soon as the graft has taken and is growing well.

In the wild, quandongs grow by seeding and there is naturally a large variation within the species. This could be exploited by choosing seedling trees with the largest, sweetest fruits and good cropping potential to graft onto seedling rootstocks.

Pests and diseases

Like most Australian native plants there are several species of insects that may chew the leaves or live on these plants but I have heard of none that are a real problem.

Harvesting and use

Round fruits up to 7 cm are produced and they are fleshy, bright red or orange–red. The flesh, which is slightly acidic and tart, is often made into sweets, and is wonderful for making jams, pies and stews, and can be dried to store for long periods. The quandong fruit itself can also be dried and kept for long periods. There are now a growing number of commercial quandong ventures, mostly dealing in the fruit.

Most attention has been paid to the quandong fruit but the trees could also be grown for their unique nuts, currently being investigated for their potential as a marketable nut species. The quandong seed (nut) is unique in that it is round and has a very indented, lumpy surface. I remember as a child playing Chinese Checkers and the 'marbles' used in this game were actually quandong seeds. The dried seeds are also used as necklaces and ornaments. The seed kernel of the nut is edible and can be eaten raw or roasted. Quandong nuts have a very high vitamin C content and contain up to 70% oil. They cannot yet be recommended for human consumption until further research is carried out, especially as they are not very palatable because of the methyl benzoate in the kernels (which decreases over storage time).

Water Chestnuts

Eleocharis dulcis

The water chestnut is not well known in Australia but many people have unknowingly eaten the so-called 'nuts' from this plant in such dishes as Chinese stir-fries. The solid crunchy pieces are usually small portions of water chestnut. Canned Chinese water chestnuts are readily available.

The water chestnut plant is rush-like in growth and usually occurs naturally in soil on flooded land or marshy swamp areas. Well-grown plants can reach one metre or more. In China, water chestnuts can be seen growing in 'paddy fields' in the same way that farmers grow rice or lotus root. The plant spreads readily but does not seem to become invasive.

The 'nutlets' harvested from the water chestnut are actually corms (see Glossary) that grow on the ends of rhizomatous (see Glossary) roots of the plant, and are produced late in the season. They are not unlike gladioli corms in that they have a rough outer layer which is peeled away. The corm revealed is creamy white and smooth and the flesh is very crisp and crunchy, with a slightly nutty taste. The typical size that is marketed (after sorting) in China is over 50 mm in diameter.

In China, where it is known as *ma tai* ('horses hooves'), the water chestnut has been cultivated for thousands of years and was probably originally bred from the wild, small-cormed species. There, the plant is commonly called a nut but is classified as a vegetable. The corms are very commonly seen in the open market places where they are sold in several ways: packaged in open mesh bags containing several corms; peeled and put on bamboo sticks 'ready to eat'; or sold loose, washed and unpeeled, from open baskets.

The water chestnut (*Eleocharis dulcis*) is available and grown in Australia, although commercial production is limited because of the labour intensive methods of harvesting. There is, however, another plant called a water chestnut, or sometimes water caltrop, and it is very important that the two plants are not confused. While the Chinese water chestnut already described belongs to the rush family (*Cyperaceae*), the water caltrop (*Trapa natans* and *T. bicornis*)) actually belongs to the water chestnut family (*Trapaceae*). The *Trapa* spp. are aquatic plants adapted for growth in water. Plants have both underwater and floating leaves. Fibrous roots develop from underwater stems. The underwater leaves are thin, narrow and deciduous whilst the floating leaves are fan-shaped with inflated stems that enable the plant to float on the water. The flowers are borne on the axils of the floating stems and produce seed pods (water chestnuts) that have also been utilised as a food source. The nuts are quite distinctive looking when fully grown, like tiny, ornately carved animal heads with horns. Before maturity the nuts are usually green coloured. Mature water chestnut seeds are hard and a black–grey colour. *T. natans* has four fused nuts with 'horns' and *T. bicornis* has only two.

Water caltrop or water chestnut (*Trapa natans*) plants are common in China and are grown in ponds and water gardens. They are highly invasive and their import into Australia is prohibited as they could escape into waterways and streams and cause untold damage, including blockage of natural water flows, creeks and rivers. They are already a major problem in the US and Canada.

Care and maintenance

Water chestnuts (*Eleocharis dulcis*) grow best planted in areas like small ponds or the edges of dams where they can be covered with 100–300 mm of water. They grow well in pots at the edges of ponds. I have had great success with water chestnuts as potted plants; the corms grew well and reproduced reasonably well, considering the fact that they were watered only intermittently, with scant regard for their need to be grown in water.

Although these plants are grown in the warmer areas of Southern China, they do best in climatic zones that have a long, sunny summer with a cool autumn–winter. They have been grown in tropical areas of Australia and I have seen them growing as far south as Kingston in Tasmania.

The plants benefit from regular applications of plant food, organic foods being preferred. Thinning of plants is rarely done because they are lifted (harvested) every year.

Pests and diseases

No pests or diseases of importance affect these plants when they are grown in Australia.

Propagation

Selected corms of the water chestnut (*Eleocharis dulcis*) are planted out in early spring into nursery beds with moist soil. Prior to planting organic fertilisers are applied to the soil. The planting distance between corms may be as close as 20 mm. They are given copious quantities of liquid

Water chestnuts (*Elicharis dulcis*) growing in paddy fields, Quilin, China

Water caltrop (*Trapa bicornis*) dried seeds and fresh water chestnuts (*Elicharis dulcis*) to show difference

manures to keep them in active growth. When plants reach about 20 mm or more they are transplanted to rows, allowing three times the original planting distance between them. Once the plants grow to about 200 mm they are transplanted to their permanent position to about one metre apart and the plots flooded with water.

During the growing season and at the stage of producing lateral rhizomes (the method the plant uses to spread) the plants are fed a mix of solid and liquid organic fertilisers including peanut cake and some wood ash (lime). Plants are usually kept in water until just before harvest which is in late autumn when early frosts will have killed the above ground parts of the plant.

Harvesting and use

Corms are usually harvested in late winter when they are at their sweetest. The water chestnut is eaten raw or cooked. One real attribute of water chestnuts is that when the corms are diced and cooked they do not lose their crisp crunchiness, they do not break down and become slushy or turn soft and their taste is maintained. These factors make them one of the most desired foods of China and the Western world. Water chestnuts are nutritious and have some medicinal value. They are low in calories and in sodium, but they contain useful amounts of potassium.

The corms of the water chestnut have a very limited life once harvested and store for only two or three weeks before wilting and deteriorating. If they are to be kept they should be placed in cool storage. They can be canned and, washed peeled, can be frozen with some success to enable longer storage.

Permaculture exponents have tried growing this both as a food plant and often as an ornamental, semi-aquatic pond plant, used as a landscape feature.

There are several cultivars of the water chestnut grown in China to suit different areas and different needs.

Further Reading

1986, *The Macquarie Dictionary of Trees and Shrubs*, Macquarie Library, Dee Why, NSW.

1995, *Horticulture Australia*, Morescope Publishing, Hawthorn East, Vic.

ABC Television, Gardening Australia, 'Plastic Surgery' (segment about grafting with Allen Gilbert), 22 October 1999.

Bailey, F.M. 1909, *Comprehensive Catalogue of Queensland Plants, both indigenous and naturalised*, Queensland Government, Brisbane.

Baker, H. 1998, *The Fruit Garden Displayed* (eighth edition), Royal Horticultural Society, London.

Baxter, P. 1991, *Fruit for Australian Gardens*, Pan Macmillan, Chippendale, NSW.

Beazley, M. 1997, *The Complete Book of Plant Propagation*, Reed International Books Ltd, London.

Bennet, P. 1989, Australia and New Zealand Organic Gardening, Child & Associates, French's Forest, NSW.

Boas, I.H. 1947, *The Commercial Timbers of Australia: Their properties and use*, Council for Scientific and Industrial Research, Melbourne.

Brock, J. 1988, *Top End Native Plants*, John Brock, Darwin.

Brock, J. 1993, *Native Plants of Northern Australia*, Reed, Chatswood, NSW.

Bryden, J.D. & Mort, C.H. 1961, *Almond Growing*, NSW Department of Agriculture (Division of Horticulture), Sydney.

Cherikoff, V. & Isaacs J. nd, *The Bush Food Handbook*, Ti Tree Press, Balmain.

Crosthwaite, I. 1994, *Peanut Growing in Australia*, DPI, Brisbane.

CSIRO 1970, *Insects of Australia*, Melbourne University Press, Melbourne.

Cundall, P. 1989, *The Practical Australian Gardener*, McPhee Gribble Penguin Books, Ringwood, Vic.

Despeissis, A. 1921, *TheHandbook of Horticulture and Viticulture of Western Australia*, WA Department of Agriculture, Perth

Edmunds, A. nd, *Espalier Fruit Trees*, Horticultural Press, Carlton.

Elliot, W.R. & Jones, D.L. 1982, *Encyclopaedia of Australian Plants suitable for cultivation*, Vol. 7, Lothian Books, Port Melbourne.

Elliot, W. R. & Jones, D. L. 1993, *Encyclopaedia of Australian Plants suitable for cultivation*, Vol. 6, Lothian Books, Port Melbourne.

Elliot, W.R. & Jones, D.L. 1997, *Encyclopaedia of Australian Plants suitable for cultivation*, Vol. 2, Lothian Books, Port Melbourne.

Ellis, B.W. & Bradley, F.M. 1996, *The Gardener's Handbook of Natural Insect and Disease Control*, Rhodale Press, Emmaus, Pennsylvania, USA.

Gilbert, A. 1991, *Yates Green Guide to Gardening: A no fuss guide to organic gardening*, Angus & Robertson/HarperCollins, Pymble NSW.

Gilbert, A. 1992, *No Garbage: Composting and recycling*, Lothian Books, Melbourne.

Gilbert, A. 2001, *All About Apples*, Hyland House, Melbourne.

Gilbert, A. 2001, *Organic Gardening for the Home Garden* (Yates Mini Guide), HarperCollins, Pymble, NSW.

Gilbert, A. 2001, *Trees and Shrubs for the Home Garden* (Yates Mini Guide), HarperCollins, Pymble, NSW.

Glowinski, L. 1997, *The Complete Book of Fruit Growing in Australia* (updated paperback edition), Lothian Books, Port Melbourne.

Goode, J. & Willson, C. 1987, *Fruit and*

Vegetables of the World, Lothian Publishing Company, Port Melbourne.

Garner, R.J. 1947, *The Grafter's Handbook*, Cassell Publishers Ltd, London.

Hely, P.C. et al. 1982, *Insect Pests of Fruit and Vegetables in NSW*, Inkata Press, Melbourne.

Hibbert, M. 2002, *The Aussie Plant Finder 2002 for 2*, Florilegium, Glebe.

Holmgren, David 2002, *Permaculture: Principles and pathways beyond sustainability*, Holmgren Design Services, Hepburn, Vic.

Isaacs, J. 1987, *Bush Food: Aboriginal food and herbal medicine*, Weldons, McMahons Point, NSW.

Janson, H.F. 1996, *Pomona's Harvest: An illustrated chronicle of antiquarian fruit literature*, Timber Press, Portland, Oregon.

Jaynes, R.A. ed. 1981, *Nut Tree Culture in North America*, Northern Nut Growers Association, Inc., Hamden, Connecticut.

Jones, D.L. 1986, *Ornamental Rainforest Plants in Australia*, Reed Books, French's Forest, NSW.

Kains, M.G. & McQuesten, L.M. 1942, *Propagation of Plants*, Orange Judd Publishing Co. Inc., New York.

L.H. Bailey Hortorium Cornell University 1976, *Hortus Third: A concise dictionary of plants cultivated in the United States and Canada*, Macmillan Publishing, New York.

Lord, E.E. 1967, *Shrubs and Trees for Australian Gardens*, Lothian Publishing, Melbourne.

Malins, J. 1992, *The Essential Pruning Companion*, David & Charles, Devon, UK.

McMaugh, J. 2001, *What Garden Pest or Disease is That?* New Holland Publishers, Sydney.

Mitchell, A.F. 1972, *Conifers in the British Isles: A descriptive handbook* (Forestry Commission booklet No 33), HMSO, London.

Mollison, B. 1991, *Introduction to Permaculture*, Tagari Publications, Sydney.

Nicholson, N. & Nicholson, H. 1991, *Australian Rainforest Plants II* (second edition), Hugh and Nan Nicholson, The Channon, NSW.

Nicholson, N. & Nicholson, H. 1992, *Australian Rainforest Plants* (fourth edition), Hugh and Nan Nicholson, The Channon, NSW.

Nicholson, N. & Nicholson, H. nd, *Australian Rainforest Plants III*, Hugh and Nan Nicholson, The Channon, NSW.

Page, P.E. 1984, *Tropical Tree Fruits for Australia*, Queensland Department of Primary Industries, Brisbane.

Rodd, Tony (chief consultant) 1997, *Botanica*, Random House, Milson's Point, NSW.

Rodd, Tony (chief consultant) 1999, *Botanica's Pocket Annuals and Perennials*, Random House, Milson's Point, NSW.

Rodd, Tony (chief consultant) 1999, *Botanica's Pocket Trees and Shrubs*, Random House, Milson's Point, NSW.

Sanders, T.W. 1964, *Sander's Encyclopaedia of Gardening* (revised by A.G. L. Hellyer), W.H. & L. Collingridge, Florida.

Stewart, A. 1999, *Let's propagate: A plant propagation manual for Australia*, ABC Books, Sydney.

Usher, G. 1971, *A Dictionary of Plants used by Man*, Constable, London.

Valder P. 1999, *The Garden Plants of China*, Florilegium, Glebe.

Wee Yeow Chin & Hsuan Keng 1990, *An Illustrated Dictionary of Chinese Medicinal Herbs*, Times Editions, Singapore.

William, K.A.W. 1979, *Native Plants of Queensland, Vol. 1*, Keith A.W. Williams, Ipswich.

William, K.A.W. 1987, *Native Plants of Queensland, Vol. 3*, Keith A.W. Williams, Ipswich.

William, K.A.W. 1988, *Native Plants of Queensland, Vol. 2* (second edition), Keith A.W. Williams, Ipswich.

Wilson, E.E. & Ogawa, J.M. 1979, *Fungal, Bacterial and Certain Nonparasitic Diseases of Fruit and Nut Crops in California*, University of California, Los Angeles.

Wright, J.I. 1983, *Plant Propagation for the Amateur Gardener*, Blandford Press, Poole.

Resources

Peak organic industry body in Australia

Organic Federation Australia, 452 Lygon St., East Brunswick, Vic. 3057.
Tel. 03 9386 6600. Fax 03 9384 1322.
www.ofa.org.au.

Certification bodies

Australian Quarantine Inspection Service (AQIS), GPO Box 858, Canberra ACT 2601.
Tel. 02 6272 3933. Freecall 1800 020 504.
www.aqis.gov.au.

Biodynamic Research Institute, Main Road, Powelltown, Vic. 3797.
Tel/fax 03 5966 7333.

Biological Farmers of Australia (BFA), PO Box 3404, Toowoomba Village Fair, 456 Ruthven St., Toowoomba, Qld. 4350.
Tel. 07 4369 3299. Fax 07 4639 3755.
www.bfa.com.au

Eco-organics of Australia, PO Box 198, Coraki, NSW 2471. Tel. 02 6625 1500.
Fax 02 6683 2815.

National Association for Sustainable Agriculture (NASAA), PO Box 768, Stirling, SA 5152. Tel. 08 8370 8455.
Fax 08 8370 8381. www.nasaa.com.au

Organic Food Chain, PO Box 2390, Toowoomba, Qld. 4350. Tel. 07 4637 2600.
Fax 4696 7689.

Organic Herb Growers of Australia Inc., PO Box 6171, South Lismore, NSW 2480.
Tel. 02 6629 1057.
www.organicherbs.org.au

Organic Vignerons Association Australia, PO Box 503, Nuriootpa, SA 5355.
Tel. 08 8562 2122. Fax 08 8562 3034.

Nut organisations and resources

Almondco Australia Limited, PO Box 1744, Sturt Highway, Renmark, SA 5341.
Tel. 08 8595 1770. Fax 08 8595 1559.
www.almondco.com.au

Australian Almond Growers Association Inc., P O Box 52, Berri, SA 5343.

Australian Nut Industry Council.
PO Box 621, Renmark, SA 5341.
Tel. 08 8586 3588. Fax 08 8586 3588.
www.nutindustry.org.au.
ANIC is a federation of all the Australian nut producing industries.

Australian Pioneer Pistachio Company, PO Box 1278, Potts Point, NSW 2011.
Tel. 02 9906 7606. Fax 02 9966 4141.
www.aus-pistachio.com.au

Australian Quandong Industry Association Inc., PO Box 1160, Loxton, SA 5333.

Chestnut Growers of Australia Limited, PO Box 4, Chiltern, Vic. 3683.
www. chestnutgrowers.com.au

Hazelnut Growers of Australia Limited, PO Box 321, Bathurst, NSW 2795.
Tel. 0500 829 357. www.hazelnuts.org.au

Australian Macadamia Society Ltd, Suite 1, 113 Dawson St, Lismore, NSW 2480.
www.macadamias.org.au

Australian Pecan Growers Association Inc., PO Box 590, Lismore, NSW 2480. information bulletin ($40) Pecan Information, PO Box 590, Lismore, NSW 2480

Pistachio Growers Association Inc.
PO Box 951, Renmark, SA 5341.

Australian Walnut Industry Association, 5 Rolls Court, Glen Waverley, Vic. 3150.
Tel/fax 03 9802 8670.
Freecall 1800 635 510

Other useful organisations

Australian National Botanic Gardens,
GPO Box 1777, Canberra, ACT 2601.
Tel. 02 6250 9450. www.anbg.gov.au/anbg

Bio-Dynamic Farming and Gardening
Association Australia Inc., PO Box 54,
Bellingen, NSW 2454.
Tel. 02 6655 0566. Fax 02 6655 0565.
www.biodynamics.net.au

Cygnet Farm Nut Hut, 59 Skyfarm Road,
Cygnet, Tasmania 7112.
Tel/fax 03 6297 8155

Henry Doubleday Research Association,
816 Comleroy Rd, Kurrajong, NSW 2758.
Tel. 02 4576 1220. www.hdra.asn.au

Holmgren Design Services, 16 Fourteenth St,
Hepburn, Vic. 3461. Tel. 03 5348 3636.
www.spacountry.net.au/holmgren/

Horticulture Australia, Level 1 50 Carrington
St, Sydney, NSW 2000.
Tel. 02 8295 2300. Fax 02 8295 2399.
www.horticulture.com.au

Institue for Horticultural Development
(IHD), Department of Primary Industries
Victoria, Private Mail Bag 15, Ferntree
Gully Delivery Centre, Vic. 3156.
Tel. 03 9210 9222. Fax 03 9800 3521.
www.nre.vic.gov.au/agvic/ihd/

Kanangra Propagators, PO Box 19B, Douglas
Park, NSW 2569. Tel/fax 02 4632 7297.
(Suppliers of grafted pistachio trees)

Permaculture International, PO Box 6039,
Lismore, NSW 2480.
www.nor.com.au/environment/perma

Permaculture Research Institute,
c/- PO Box, The Channon, NSW 2480.
Tel. 02 6688 6222. Fax. 02 6688 6499.
www.permaculture.org.au

SEED (Sustainability, Education and Ecologi-
cal Design) International, 50 Crystal Waters,
Kilcoy Lane, Conondale, Qld 4552.
Tel/Fax 07 5494 4833.
www.permaculture.au.com

South Australian Research and Development
Institute, GPO Box 397, Adelaide, SA
5001. Tel. 08 8303 9419.
Fax. 08 8303 9424. www.sardi.sa.gov.au

Sunraysia Nursery and Garden Centre,
Murray Vale Hwy, Golgol, NSW 2738.
Tel. 03 5024 8502. Fax 03 5024 8551.
www.sunraysianurseries.com.au

Sydney Postharvest Laboratory, CSIRO Food
Science Australia Building, 11 Julius Ave,
Riverside Corporate Park, Delhi Rd, North
Ryde, Sydney, NSW 2113 (PO Box 62,
North Ryde, NSW 1670).
Tel. 02 9490 8443. Fax 02 9490 8499.
www.postharvest.com.au

The Food Forest, PO Box 859, Gawler, SA
5118. Tel/fax 08 8522 6450.
www.users.bigpond.com/brookman

WWOOF (Willing Workers on Organic
Farms), Buchan, Vic. 3885.
Tel. 03 5155 0218. www.wwoof.com.au

Useful publications

Acres Australia, Freepost1, PO Box 27,
Eumundi, Qld 4562. Tel. 07 5449 1881.
Fax 07 5449 1889. Toll free 1800 801 467.
www.acresaustralia.com.au

Australian Horticulture, Rural Press Magazines,
PO Box 254, Moonee Ponds, Vic. 3039.
Tel. 03 9287 0900. Fax 03 9370 5622

Australian Nutgrower Journal, PO Box 1,
Dargo, Vic. 3862. Tel. 03 5140 1258.
Fax 03 5140 1211.

Earth Garden, PO Box 2, Trentham, Vic. 3458.
Fax 03 5424 1743.
www.earthgarden.com.au

Daley's Fruit Tree Nursery, *Australian Sub-
tropical Fruit and Nut Tree Catalogue*.
Available from Daley's Fruit Tree Nursery,
PO Box 154, via Kyogle, NSW 2474.
Tel. 02 66 321 441. fax 02 66 322 585.
www.daleysfruit.com.au

Gardening Australia, GPO Box 9994, Hobart,
Tas. 7001. Tel. 1300 656 933.
www.abc.net.au

Grass Roots, Night Owl Publications,
PO Box 242, Euroa, Vic. 3666.
Tel. 03 5794 7285

Green Connections, Po Box 793, Castlemaine,
Vic. 3450.
Tel. 03 5470 5040. Fax 03 5470 6947.
www.greenconnections.com.au

Greenhouse Living, Grass Roots Publishing,
PO Box 117, Seymour, Vic. 3661.
Tel. 03 5792 4000. Fax 03 5792 4222

Greenworld, Glenvale Publications,
PO Box 347, Glen Waverley, Vic. 3150.
Tel. 03 9544 2233. Fax 03 9543 1150.

The Organic Gardener, PO Box 1067,
Lismore, NSW 2480. Tel. 1300 656 933.

Useful websites

Asian Food Information Centre (AFIC) (non-profit, based in Singapore) www.afic.org/

Association of Societies for Growing Australian Plants (ASGAP) www.farrer.riv.csu.edu.au/ASGAP

Australian New Crops newsletter, www.newcrops.uq.edu.au/newslett/

California Pistachio Commission, www.pistachios.org/

Earthcare Enterprises, plant information and nursery Queensalnd, www.earthcare.com.au

International Macadamias Ltd. (based in Australia) www.macadamia.au.com

International Tree Nut Council (based in Spain) www.inc.treenuts.org

Pennsylvania Nut Growers Association, www.pnga.net/

University of California Fruit and Nut Research Information Centre, www.fruitsandnuts.ucdavis.edu/

Glossary

Acidic: soil, water or liquid or the taste of a thing is said to be acidic when it has an acid-like consistency or taste, and a low acidity reading. This is measured by an acidity/alkalinity pH meter with range from 0–14, and a reading below pH 7 is considered acidic.

Aerial layering is a plant propagation method based on propagating from a stem or branch piece while the branch is still attached to the tree. It involves cutting the stem or removing a section of bark and sometimes applying rooting substances to the injured part. The stem can then be wrapped with moss, tissue, or similar soft substance and then wrapped in foil or plastic. When roots develop the branch is cut off and planted out in a pot or in the ground (see also Marcotting in this Glossary).

Aflatoxins are poisonous products produced by fungal organisms of the Aspergillus spp. which can infect some nuts and their products.

Aflatoxicosis is the medical term for the condition experienced when poisoned by aflatoxins. In Western developed countries it most usually occurs in animals, and acute symptoms can include necrosis (death of tissue or an organ), cirrhosis and cancer of the liver.

Alkaline: an alkaline product, liquid or soil has a high pH reading, above pH 7, and may have a slimy but corrosive taste.

Apical dominance refers to the topmost bud on the tallest shoot or the tallest shoot of an upright lateral that grows fast and strong, inhibiting growth from lower buds. This is often used to advantage when training nut trees to a central leader system.

Auxins are hormone-like materials used for promoting plant growth. An example is Gibberellic acid.

Basal heating is applying heat or providing warmth at the bottom of cuttings or a propagating tray/pot.

Biennial bearing is how a tree or plant is described when it bears fruit one year but hardly any the next. This condition can be overcome by using my new pruning system as well as by using other pruning methods.

Bonsai is the art of miniaturising trees by constant pruning and root pruning and containing their growth in tiny pots as potted plants.

Branch refers to the main structural arms of a tree.

Budding is the act of placing a bud under the bark of a rootstock tree or inserting a chip bud into a rootstock to produce a tree or branch bearing a selected cultivar.

Bud scales are usually grey, tiny, scale-like, scalloped tissue, that enclose a dormant leaf or flower bud.

Bud union is that point where the bud has been inserted or a scion grafted to the stock plant and usually shows as a change in bark characteristics such as a slight swelling or bending of the trunk, or a scarred tissue area. It is usually about 100–300 mm above soil level on standard trees or well above ground on high-trunked trees such as weeping standards.

Callus tissue is formed from the cambium layer and is the lumpy growth that precedes roots on nut cuttings grown from evergreen shoots or shortened dormant laterals. Callusing also occurs around the graft area of the tree, around injury sites, or on cut limb-ends and, in this case, the word 'callusing' refers to the formation of scar-like yellow or cream-coloured tissue at the edge of and around the graft joint.

Cambium layer is an indeterminate layer just under the bark where the healing tissue needed for a successful graft or bud is situated.

Catkins are tiny male flowers usually in a hanging, round, tubular-like structure. They produce pollen to pollinate female flowers. Some of the main tree nuts produce male catkins for pollination.

Central leader refers to a centrally trained branch that is allowed to grow or is pruned to produce a central leader shaped tree.

Chamfer means to cut a sharp edge at an angle, thus creating a sloped, cut edge. On a cut limb this is done to bark level to lessen the pressure of the bark and allow easier callusing to occur on its end.

Chip budding refers to the placing of a chip-shaped bud from one plant to another to propagate a particular cultivar.

Chunk pruning refers to pruning by random selection of pieces of branch and spur systems.

Cincturing is making a cut or placing a stricture into the bark layer around a limb or branch to upset the flow of sap (see also *notching*). The purpose of cincturing is to direct the flow of nutrients to the fruiting parts of the tree and to fool the tree into thinking it is damaged and should get on with fruiting.

Compost is material derived from the degradation and breakdown of organic materials.

Cordon is the name given to a tree trained as a single trunk that is usually planted on an angle.

Corms are bulb-like structures produced by plants for self-propagation. Corms have a solid centre with growth buds on the outside, compared to true bulbs which have a growth point in the centre of the bulb.

Cotyledon refers to the, usually two, protective pseudo leaves that surround the embryo of a seed such as the almond. When the seed is germinated the cotyledons are the first to grow and expand, providing food for the developing shoot. The cotyledons are the first part of the plant to appear at germination and look like two leaves with a tiny central growth point.

Cross pollination is induced when pollen from different trees pollinates the flowers of a

given tree. Pollen for cross pollination can be supplied by a branch of flowers (or catkins) placed into a nut tree, by flowers on an attached graft or by a nearby tree. Pollen is usually transferred by wind, insects or bees. Some fruit trees are self-pollinating.

Crop supports are used to support some branches of nut trees when they are heavily laden with fruit. Gardeners can use support sticks, crutches or sticks if they think the crop will be heavy enough to break the branches.

Crotch refers to the angle that a limb makes with its major branches or trunk.

Cull is a term used to refer to the removal of sick, unhealthy or diseased plants.

Cultivar is a nut selection that has been deliberately bred or selected by plant breeders using various plant breeding techniques. These nuts can be registered under the Plant Variety Act (PVR) and persons selling the scions or buds from this plant can obtain a royalty for every nut tree of that cultivar that is produced under Plant Breeders Rights (PBR).

Dormancy is the period when deciduous plants that lose leaves in autumn have no leaves and no apparent growth occurring. Some evergreen trees (and nuts) are said to have a period of dormancy when they cease growth at any time.

Drupe is a fruit. The classic drupe is a one or more seeded fruit that has the seeds inside a hard layer (stone or shell) and a fleshy or leathery outer layer (such as almonds).

Espalier: an espalier system is a method of training trees flat against a wall, upon a frame or trellis system. Espaliers can also be trained to be free standing.

Etiolation refers to the partial or total exclusion of light from a growing plant. This is usually done for 'stock' plants that are to be used for cuttings or for grafting material. The plant is put back into full sunlight for one or two weeks prior to taking cuttings or scions from it. Etiolation increases the percentage take of cuttings and the success of grafted *scions*.

Flesh refers to the inside edible part of the nut under the skin.

Flower buds of nut trees differ from cultivar to cultivar, but in general flower buds are larger than leaf buds and are rotund and round at the centre like a Buddha. Flower buds can occur upon new growth laterals or on second- and third-year-old wood. Spur systems on deciduous trees containing flower buds once developed continue to grow spurs for the life of the tree, or until the spur system dies. New buds can be forced to grow from very old branches by hard pruning or by partial *cincturing* (see above) and then allowing those shoots to remain unpruned to produce flower buds. A flower spur is a short growth under 100 mm long with a terminal flower bud.

Foliar fertiliser is fertiliser used in liquid form and applied by spraying onto plant foliage.

Frass is the name given to material excreted by insects as they digest plant matter.

Fruit maturity is when fruit is mature enough to pick.

Fruit spurs are short growths 1–5 cm long containing flower buds. They often occur in clusters.

Grafting is the transfer of a bud or *scion* from a selected *cultivar* to a chosen *rootstock* tree.

Heeling in refers to the temporary burying of bare-rooted trees in soil to keep the roots moist and prevent them drying out.

Humus is a product produced during composting. It must be noted that humus is not *compost*.

Internode is the name given to the distance between one leaf and the next on a growth *lateral*.

Laterals are short new shoots longer than 100 mm that grow from around the pruning sites and from all over the tree. In traditional pruning systems for deciduous trees, such as the open vase method, almost all the laterals are removed during the winter pruning operation, leaving a bare, open, widely spaced, branched vase shape with no scraggy or long shoots anywhere upon the tree. My method, in contrast, leaves somewhat scraggy, long, bent shoots all over the tree frame so that there is no space where you can observe wide sections of daylight through the limb structure.

When laterals are removed from the tree, others will grow from the base of the cut area. If laterals are cut in half they often produce flower buds and shoots. Sometimes (in most cases) they just produce a group of more long laterals. I have found that if a lateral is left unpruned it will develop *spur* growth all along that lateral during the next spring–summer growth period. Utilising this factor, gardeners can adapt their tree to a partial non-pruning system and get far better results than they do when removing all laterals, or they can completely convert the tree to my new pruning system.

Lateral roots are the roots that grow sideways from the tree root system.

Layering is the bending of growing shoots of a plant into soil or a soil medium, covering a section of them (sometimes injuring or removing a section of bark from the bent point of the stem piece). Root formation occurs at the point that is covered with soil.

Leaching (of the soil) happens when water percolates through the soil, dissolving salts and nutrients and carrying them to the subsoil or into the water table.

Leader is the term given to the top of any main branch or sub-branch forming the basic framework of the pruning system used, i.e. a vase shaped tree may have 8-15 leaders forming the vase shape.

Leaf buds produce leaves and shoots only and are a flattened triangular shape. Leaf buds can be produced on all parts of the tree but are predominant all along new *lateral* growths with a pointed terminal leaf bud. Often the laterals will have leaf buds only and are situated at the base of any leaf on the lateral. New laterals with leaf buds are often chosen to supply *scions* and buds for *budding* and *grafting* operations. A leaf spur is a short growth under 100 mm long with a terminal leaf bud. If this spur is left unpruned the leaf bud spur usually changes into a flower bud spur during the next season. Leaf buds on evergreen trees are found at the base of leaf stalks and at the tip growth.

Marcotting is a form of *aerial layering* that begins by removing a section of bark from a twig or branch. A material such as moist sphagnum moss is then wrapped around this area and the whole lot is enclosed in plastic or aluminium foil to seal it. Roots grow from the wound area into the moss, then the branch is severed and placed into a pot. Some plants such as lychees are best propagated by this method.

Multi graft is the placing a few or many grafts on the one *rootstock* or tree.

Mutation is when a section of growth with

apparently different nuts occurs naturally on a given tree. Sometimes this is caused by ultra violet rays, cell mutation, viral infection, or environmental conditions. Mutations may be skin deep, change the whole nut or create colouration or different shaped leaves.

Natural fruit drop or shedding occurs as the fruits start to develop internal seeds. If the seeds do not form properly then the young fruitlets will drop from the tree. Natural sheddng of fruit (nuts) can occur because of the number of nuts on heavily laden trees, the nutrient status of the tree, trees being too vigorous, water availability or other factors, but it is a normal occurrence.

Nematodes are very small, worm-like creatures that cannot usually be seen with the naked eye. Some are pathogenic and feed on plants, causing damage to tissue or roots.

Notching (or partial cincturing) is the action of placing a small cut in a tree limb or branch to initiate shoot growth (see also *cincturing*).

Nut shapes vary with varieties and *cultivars* and sometimes with climate. Nuts can be conical, round, oblong, squarish, teardrop shape, flattened or oval.

Pink bud refers to the stage when pink or white just-opening almond flower buds can be seen on the tree.

Petiole is the stalk of a leaf.

PVR (Plant Variety Rights) allows a plant breeder to register newly bred plants and to receive royalties from the sale of propagation material of that plant.

PBR (Plant Breeders Rights) is the name given to the right to obtain royalties from plant material which has been bred by a particular plant breeder. For example, a person who has developed a new nut cultivar by cross breeding receives royalties under PBR every time the plant is propagated for sale.

Pistil is the female part of flower that receives pollen and usually shows as a short, rod-like structure.

Pistilate means flowers with female structure.

Plant naming, or nomenclature, is based on a uniform system that owes much of its origins to the work of the great Swedish naturalist, Linnaeus (1707–78). The angiosperms, the major flowering plant group on earth, are divided into two main groups, the dicotyledons (having two *cotyledons* or seed leaves) and the monocotyledons (having one cotyledon). Both groups are then further subdivided into orders, families, genera and species, with a species being a group of plants with the closest similarities and the most distinct and very specific characteristics. Genera are groups of related species while families are groups of related genera and so on for orders of plants. The genus *Prunus*, for example, contains all the species of stone fruit (e.g. peaches, apricots, nectarines, plums and almonds). A species within this group is, for example, the almond *Prunus amygdalus*.

Naming conventions are quite strict. Each species has a common name (or a number of common names) and a botanical name and, while common names may vary, the botanical name generally does not (although a species can have synonymous names, and names can be changed when, for example, new information leads to a reclassification of a species). The botanical name for each species consists of a combination of its genus and species names, e.g. the almond is identified botanically as *Prunus amygdalus* with *Prunus* being the genus name and *amygdalus* being the species name.

How botanical names are written also has strict rules. They are usually written in italics, with the genus name first and capitalised, the species name second and not capitalised. A species name can also have a subspecies included (e.g. the blue gum *Eucalyptus globulus* ssp. *globulus*) or a species can have a variety (named cultivar) name attached to it as is common in the case of such species as roses (e.g. *Rosa roxburghii* 'Plena'). To complicate naming conventions, variety names are not italicised and are enclosed in inverted commas. There are many other rules and conventions but these are the most common.

These conventions are not always as well adhered to as they might be and this can lead to confusion. It is important to use correct botanical names wherever possible to make sure that plants are identified correctly.

Pleaching occurs when branches cross one another and form a graft.

Pollen donor is the term used to describe the nut tree providing pollen to enable cross pollination to occur.

Pollinator is a plant used to supply pollen so
that sufficient pollination can occur to
produce good crops.

Pollination occurs when male pollen is transferred to a female flower.

Proboscis is a hollow, needle-like part of some
insects' mouth parts and is used for sucking.

Rhizome: a rhizome is a swollen rootstock stem
of a plant that acts as a new root system
which the plant uses to self-propagate. The
rhizone may contain shoots or buds along
its length. A piece of this system with
growth bud or shoot attached can usually
be cut from the plant and used to increase
plant numbers. Irises are an example of
plants that grow from rhizomes.

Rod refers to a single growth or a one-branched
young tree, or to a maiden tree.

Rootstock is the chosen plant onto which to
bud or graft a known variety or cultivar of
nut and it provides the roots for the nut
tree. Often particular rootstocks have distinct advantages such as being disease
resistant, having a dwarfing effect, or being
capable of forming a better root system for
the grafted plant.

Scion refers to a piece of *lateral* of a known
cultivar used to graft onto a *rootstock*.

Secondary leader is a sub branch that grows
from one of the main *leader* branches (see
above).

Seedling variation refers to the fact that nuts,
if grown from seed, produce hundreds of
plants growing similar types of nuts to the
parent plants, but many, although genetically similar, produce nuts that are entirely
different in size, colour, taste, or ripening
habit. In other words they do not grow 'true
to type'. The seedling variations may be
chosen as new cultivars.

Self-fertile trees have the ability to use their
own pollen for *pollination* and do not require
another tree for pollination to occur.

Self-infertile is used to describe a species when
the pollen from a given tree cannot be used
to pollinate its own flowers; another donor
(cultivar) is usually needed.

Self-pollination refers to pollen transfer between
flowers of one cultivar on one tree and its
own flowers.

Sport: this is a naturally occurring *mutation* on
a tree or a shoot or bud that gives rise to a
different characteristic, and often to spur-

forming varieties of entirely new varieties
of nuts.

Spur usually describes short growths under
100 mm in length, with or without flower
buds. Some gardeners call particular growths
spurs only if the growth shoots are under
50 mm long. Most deciduous tree pruning
systems utilise the fact that thin shoots cut
back hard will eventually throw out or
grow some flower buds on spurs. If one spur
with one flower bud is left unpruned it will
usually also produce one or two new spurs
from near the base of the original flower
bud. The production of extra spurs seems
to happen more readily on fruiting spur
clusters. Once this spur site has developed
a few spurs it is called a *spur system* and
usually remains that way for the life of the
tree (see below).

Spur pruning is to prune to initiate spur growth
and to thin out tangled or weakened *spur
systems*.

Spur systems, with flower buds developed
through pruning or non-pruning methods,
are a collection of short growths bunched
together (or single) along a *lateral*, limb or
branch (see *spurs*) especially on deciduous
trees. Because spur systems continue to grow
more spurs, these spur systems need to be
thinned out by one third every now and
then (every 5–10 years) as they do become
weakened. An individual weakened spur is
usually about half the size and diameter of
a healthy one; it will still flower but will
not set fruit. This is why spur thinning is
necessary once the system builds up or is
ageing. All systems of pruning will lead to
the development of spur systems along the
branches. Branches of very old trees can
develop to be completely covered in spurs
and not have any lateral growth at all.

Stratification is a method of laying seeds in
layers within a medium such as damp sand.
It is a method used to keep seeds moist and
to apply a cool period which will help the
seeds germinate.

Taproot is the root formed from a seedling tree
root growth and it grows straight downwards
whereas lateral roots grow from the side of
the taproot. Taproots of young trees can be
cut back to the side lateral roots at planting
time although this is not encouraged for
some species of nuts with very strong root

systems as it reduces too much the vigour of the developing plant.

Throw off (abort): this occurs if a plant is under stress from drought or other factors and means that a tree will drop developing nuts or fruits.

Tip bearing is the term used when a nut tree bear fruits only on the ends of long *laterals*. To overcome this condition summer pruning of young shoots is recommended

Tip pruning often refers to the removal of a small amount of growth from the top end of a new lateral growth, and results in removing the terminal bud from the nut lateral. The method is often used to shape young trees as more *laterals* develop under the cut area. Continued tip pruning of mature trees encourages more lateral growth (as with lychee nut trees) and will eventually form a tree rounded in shape with all the fruiting wood on the outside canopy only. The centre of the tree will not produce much fruit because the shading effect of tip pruning will kill off all inside spur systems.

Tissue culture is the propagation of a given *cultivar* of plant using only very small immature buds or pieces of plant tissue from which to propagate and involves growing these sections on to multiply them, making them produce multiple shoots and roots. These are grown under sterile conditions in flasks and once the tiny plantlets have formed they are separated and grown on to become mature specimens.

Topiary is the act of pruning and shaping trees and shoots into geometric forms or other desired shapes such as animals or birds.

Top: to top a tree is to prune its branches to prevent the tree growing any taller.

Trellis refers to a support structure upon which the nut tree is trained or tied, to obtain a set design shape.

Trunk: the trunk or trunks of a tree refer to the main supporting growths growing from soil level upwards.

Tubers are swollen roots or stems attached to some plants such as potatoes and are their means of self-propagation.

Unpruned laterals refers to the fact that pieces of new growth grown during the previous season (laterals) are left completely unpruned during the next, and sometimes subsequent, pruning season.

Variety/cultivar: a nut variety is a naturally grown nut that shows different characteristics to those of the parent plant (see *plant naming*). These can arise by *sports, mutations* and with seedling variation.

Vase shaped pruning is pruning a tree to represent an open vase shape. This is more fully described in pp. 91–101 on pruning.

Vernalisation: a period of cold needed by many plants to initiate seed germination or flower bud set.

Watershoots are very strong growing shoots that grow a metre or more during one season. They often grow from cut branches or from areas around the central base of the tree.

Whip or *whip and tongue* is a form of graft joining two pieces—*rootstock* and *scion*—together and is more fully described in pp. 71–85 on grafting.

Winter oil is an oil spray to apply to *dormant* trees. Most gardeners now use a multipurpose oil that can be applied in winter as well as in summer when there are leaves on the tree.

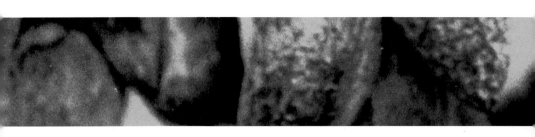

Index

Other books by
Allen Gilbert

ALL ABOUT APPLES

FULL-COLOUR, SEWN PAPERBACK
144 PAGES, 245 X 170 MM
ISBN 1 86447 046 1
$29.95

A reliable and informative guide to apples old and new, their care, control of pests and disease, propagation and harvesting.

- Includes a chapter on small-scale orcharding
- Espalier apple trees for unusual landscape effects
- Grow more than ten different apple varieties on a single tree
- Discover the beautiful taste of organic apples in many varieties from yesteryear
- More apples and less work with Allen Gilbert's pruning system

CLIMBERS AND CREEPERS

FULL-COLOUR, SEWN PAPERBACK
128 PAGES, 235 X 155 MM
ISBN 1 86447 073 9
$17.95

Let the colours, scents, and fruit of these magnificent, rambling, scrambling, crawling and sprawling plants dress up your garden!

- Clear descriptions of the best climbers and creepers
- Good colour photographs of every cultivar, so you can see how the plants you buy will look in your garden
- Australia-wide cultivation notes
- No more aimless trudging through garden nurseries

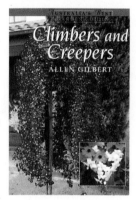

TOMATOES FOR EVERYONE

FULL-COLOUR, SEWN PAPERBACK
152 PAGES, 250 X 185 MM
ISBN 1 86447 019 4
$29.95

A Practical Guide to Growing Tomatoes All Year Round

A book for people who don't have a lot of space, time or energy, but love the taste of home-grown fruit. Share your garden with Saucy Sue, Mama's Delight, Daydream or Best of All – just a few of the many heritage tomatoes Allen shows you how to grow. Choose from hundreds of varieties, and grow them from seeds or grafts, in non-dig gardens or pots, organically or hydroponically: there's something here for everyone!